ANTHONY CARO

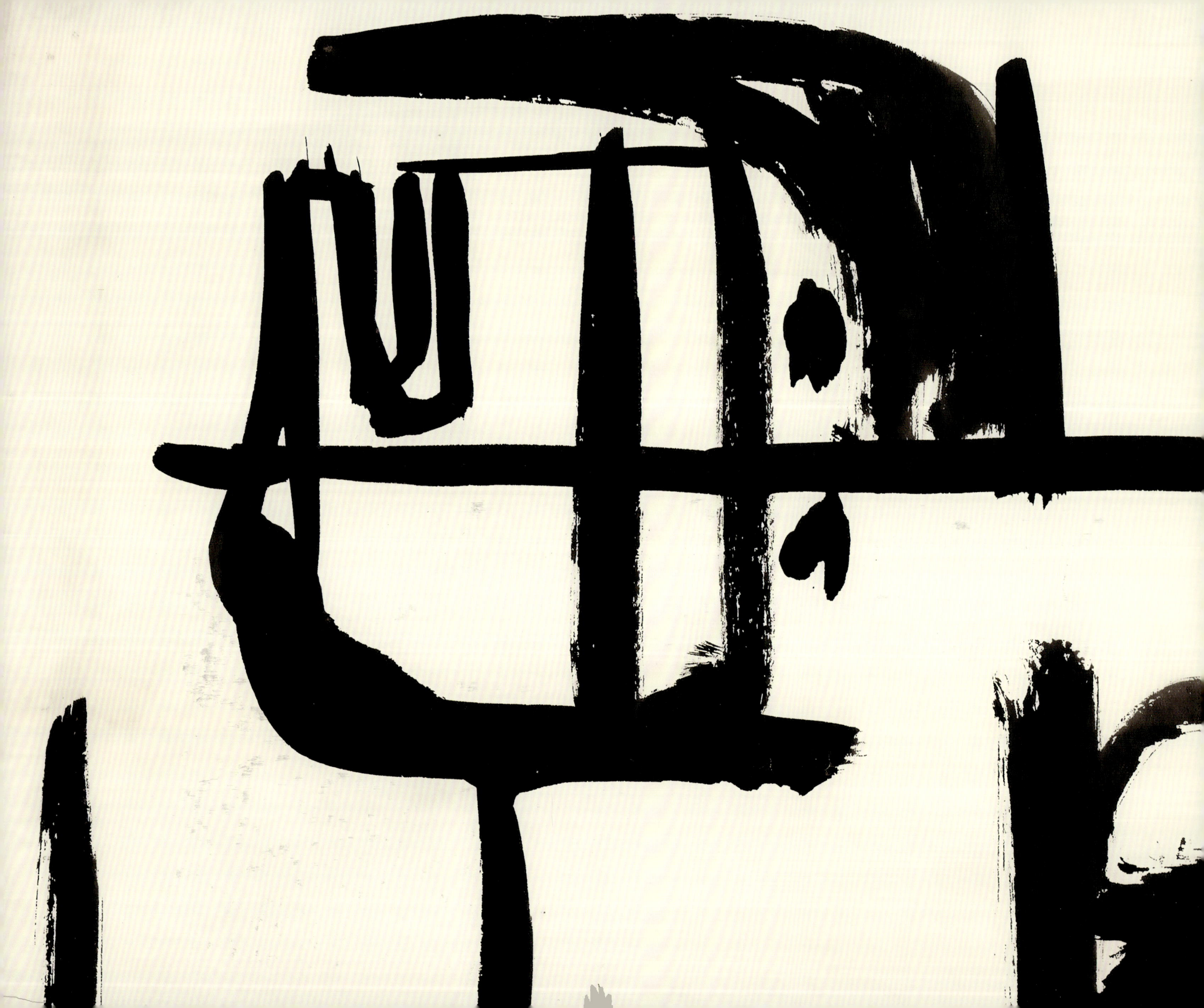

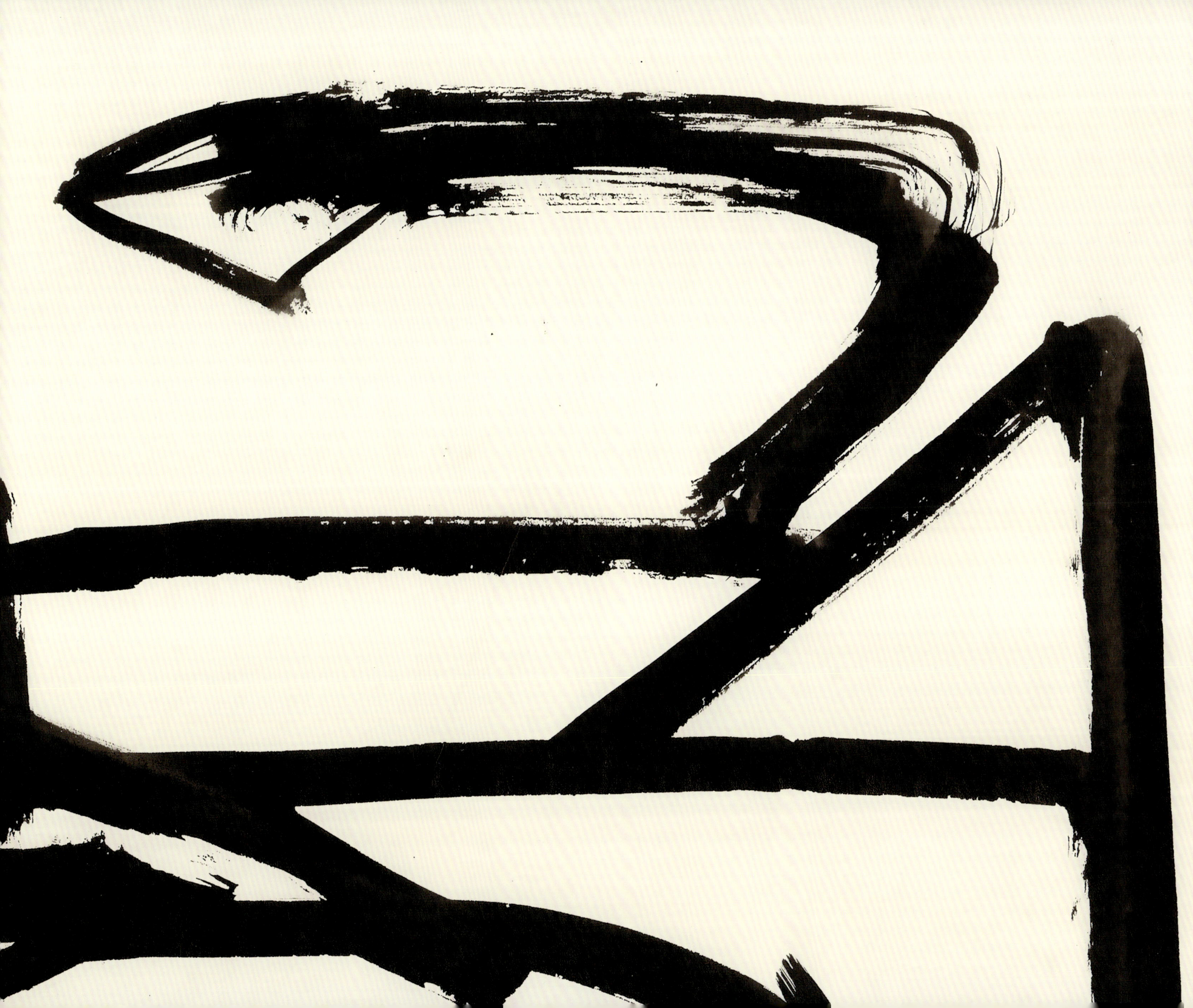

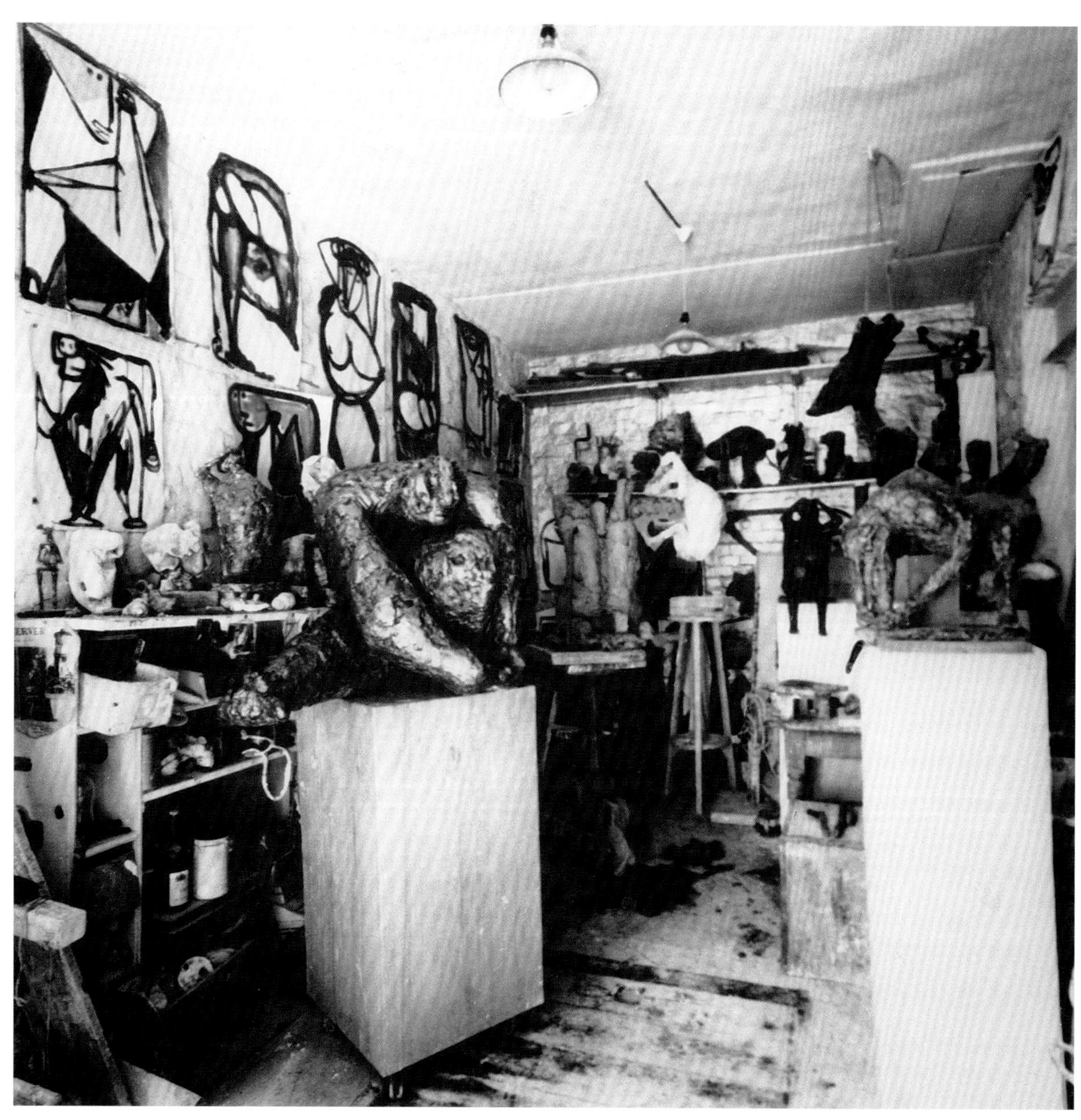

Man Holding His Foot, 1954 and *Warrior*, 1955/1956
in Caro's studio at his home in Hampstead, ca. 1955

ANTHONY CARO

first drawings last sculptures

MITCHELL-INNES & NASH
NEW YORK

FOREWARD

Lucy Mitchell-Innes

I first met Anthony Caro when I worked in his studio in the late 1970s and maintained a life-long friendship with him up until his death in 2013. I am grateful to have known him and his work over such a long period of time. The first exhibition of his sculpture I organized at Mitchell-Innes & Nash was in 2002 and featured a series known as the Barbarians. Several exhibitions and projects followed over the years with visits on both sides of the Atlantic. My last visit to the studio was just prior to his death when he had completed the Perspex sculptures on view here.

The works in this exhibition span Caro's sixty-year career from his first drawings to his last sculptures. When I first viewed these little known early works on paper, I immediately saw Tony's newer sculpture in a fresh light despite their being created more than sixty years apart. The underlying formal and conceptual links between the figuration in the works on paper and the abstraction of the Perspex sculptures was completely clear to me. Was Tony aware of these similarities? Or were they a sign of the constancy of his artistic pathway? I like to think that they were part of Tony's language and that it is only now, looking back, that we can fully appreciate his remarkable clarity of vision.

This exhibition would not have been possible without the help of Patrick Cunningham, Tony's studio manager of 47 years, whose dedication is truly invaluable. Thanks also to the team at Barford Studio, Olivia Bax and Sile Stuttard, as well as to Tony's son, Paul, who has supported this exhibition from the outset. And last but not least, I would like to thank Julius Bryant for his insightful essay which illuminates Tony's process from the early figurative drawings to the later abstract sculptures.

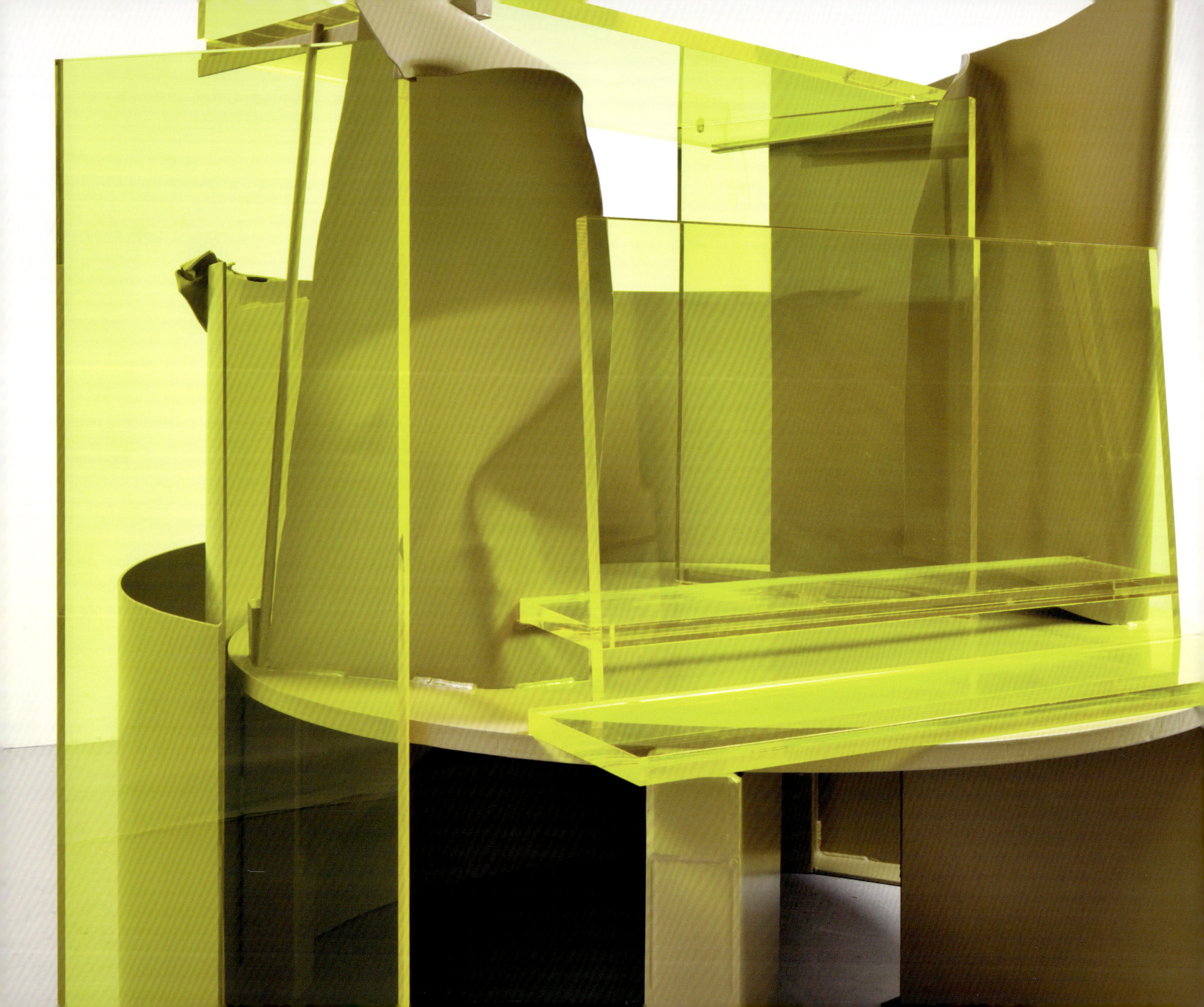

CARO ENCORE
colour and line

Julius Bryant

This is the first exhibition in New York of the work of Anthony Caro since his death in October 2013, aged eighty-nine. It presents new sculptures completed in the last months of his life, when he was experimenting with colored Perspex (known in the USA as Plexiglas). To set these sculptures in context the exhibition presents related works from much earlier in his career. In particular, it showcases three series of brushed-ink drawings from the 1950s that gave Caro fresh ideas when he studied them in 2010, for the first time in decades. The exhibition is shared between two venues. Downtown in Chelsea the larger sculptures with coloured Perspex shine alongside his coloured figure drawings, in dialogue across his sixty-year long career. Uptown, in the gallery on Madison Avenue, the focus is on his use of line with sculptures more intimate in scale from the 1970s and 1980s, shown alongside passionate expressionistic drawings from the 1950s.

Caro presented the first fruits of his experiments with coloured Perspex at the Venice Biennale in 2013, in his one-man show at the Museo Correr overlooking St. Mark's Square. While fully confident of 'working until I drop at 100' this proved to be Caro's last museum private view. Inside the Museo Correr the dividing walls enhanced the impact of each isolated work and sense of surprise, not least when one encountered Caro's debut in coloured Perspex. This newcomer stole the show. Appropriately named *Venetian*, the sculpture clearly related to the great project for New York's Park Avenue that Caro had been working on since 2009, with its longitudinal rhythms. But instead of hard red steel he had floated through it a sheet of deep translucent burgundy. Breathtaking and beguiling, like a great glaze running over darker scumblings in a Venetian portrait by Titian or Tintoretto, it seemed to sweep sheer through the steel while leaving the structure beneath still visible, but intriguing, darkened and warmed by its coloured shadow. At 89, with only weeks left, Caro had done it again, the final 'breakthrough,' but where had this new direction come from?

Caro's career could be told in terms of his changing materials. As Clement Greenberg had advised him in 1959, when he felt he had reached an impasse, 'if you want to change your art, change your habits.' Caro had worked in Perspex once before, when he made *Duccio Variations No. 5* (2000) but that was clear, not coloured, and being a one-off, had led nowhere.[1] In the history of sculpture this kind of material really belongs to Naum Gabo and his brother Antoine Pevsner. Celluloid was used creatively in sheet form by Gabo from 1916 and by Pevsner in the 1920s. (Perspex is the patent name of an acrylic plastic developed by ICI (Imperial Chemical Industries) in the 1930s.) As a young sculptor, trained at the Royal Academy in 1947-52, Caro had rejected the option of abstract sculpture; he probably had some of Gabo's Constructivist sculptures in mind when he said 'I will never make an abstract sculpture – they are empty cold things.'[2] They can indeed resemble geometric models produced by mathematicians, or perhaps the kind of three dimensional diagrams Caro had grappled with as a reluctant engineering student at Cambridge University. Caro's rediscovery of Perspex came when he saw it in colour.

Caro's appreciation of colour is often underestimated. The day Caro finished his best-known sculpture, *Early One Morning* (1962, Tate) he painted it green. His wife, Sheila Girling, immediately recognised that it had to be red, fire-engine red, and ever after Caro deferred to her when it came to colour. But he did not delegate colour away, for he knew that what comes last to the sculptor also comes first to the viewer. For a sculptor using scrap steel in collage, paint is not just a practical protection against corrosion and a means of pulling it all together, of masking

Man Holding His Foot
1954, Bronze
Height: 26 ½ inches (67.3 cm)

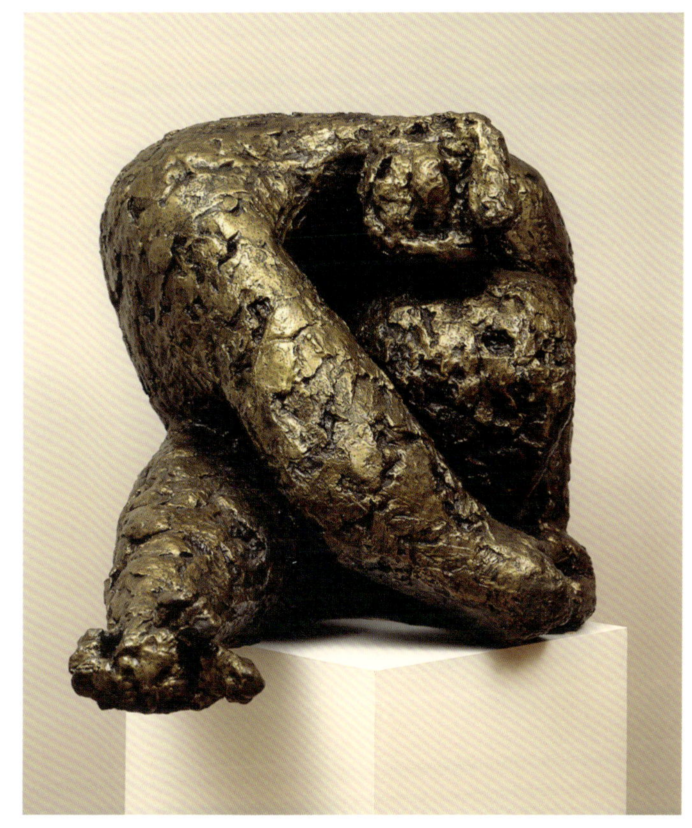

the disparate source material and the evidence of it sticking together.

Patrick Cunningham has been Caro's studio director and lead technician for 47 years, having joined him as an assistant in 1969. He knows 'when Tony needs a new material' and recalls how, while developing his most ambitious (and unrealised) sculpture, for Park Avenue, New York he became fascinated by glass. Sculptors such as Tim Scott had used clear plate glass in the 1960s, with painted wood.[3] For Caro the spark was the blue glass lining of an antique salt cellar, which Caro dropped accidentally at home and brought into work one day to get repaired. The search for a specialist took them both shopping and, following his instincts as ever, Caro gathered up glass vases and other vessels. He said at the time, 'glass interests me because it is there and not there. You see right through it but the filed edges give it presence'.[4] But the glass objects soon proved difficult as they refused to shed their source identities as domestic utensils. An example in this exhibition is *Honey Suckle* (2011-12) [pgs. 38-39], which began as an essay in wood around a tall glass bowl that in the end Caro removed. Caro had more success with glass in *Display* (2011-12) [pg. 53], a still-life of two opalesque lead-crystal cylinders divided by bronze and plate glass sheets, composed in a museum-like vitrine on a steel stand. For *Display* the cylinder shapes were cast in lead-crystal using a clay pot that Caro had made while working with the ceramicist Hans Spinner in Grasse, France.

Caro's great friend, the art historian Michael Fried, has described visiting Caro in his studio in August 2010 to see the Park Avenue series in progress and finding Caro frustrated by glass. His advice was to give up on glass objects and cast glass and try instead flat sheets of glass as 'dividers' and 'mirrors', as he had seen used by an artist in Brazil.[5] But these too proved frustrating as glass in sheet form cracked and chipped in the studio. The solution was to switch to plastic. Caro's Perspex project finally took off in 2011. But there may be another source.

One of the mantras of Modernism is that art must progress. Modernism cast its artists in the role of heroic pioneers, pushing at the frontiers of the known field, daring to go beyond the definitions and to break the rules. Caro echoed these sentiments, always caring more about the work in hand, 'never looking back.' He drew upon the history of art all his life, and at one point was confident enough to go back to life drawing and to make bronze figures.[6] But he was not one for retrospection about his own work; exhibitions were places to show something new. One day in his studio archive I was researching potential loans for a museum exhibition. There in the drawers was everything from schoolboy drawings preserved by his proud and percipient mother to life-size voluptuous life drawings in the spirit of Matisse. Most remarkable were the big colour drawings from the 1950s, the black outlines filled in with blocks of colour like stained-glass windows (e.g. *Figure,* 1955/56 [pg. 27]). They still had all the energy of Picasso's sketches towards his painting *Guernica* (1937, Centro de Arte Reina Sofia, Madrid). In the smart gallery dining room, across the yard from the studio, his son Paul and I layed them out together, with Pat. When Caro came in, at first he was amused, remarking: 'I haven't seen these in years – where did you find them?' And then he sat down in silence and stared. It was as if he was meeting his younger self and felt spellbound by his work. For an artist who famously 'never looked back' Caro was hooked. He studied the sixty-year old works spread before him with no sense of nostalgia nor need to share memories. After looking quietly for a while he just said 'I can use this.'

Paul Cézanne, *The Card Players*
1890-92, Oil on canvas
25 ¾ x 32 ¼ inches (65.4 x 81.9 cm)
The Metropolitan Museum of Art, New York

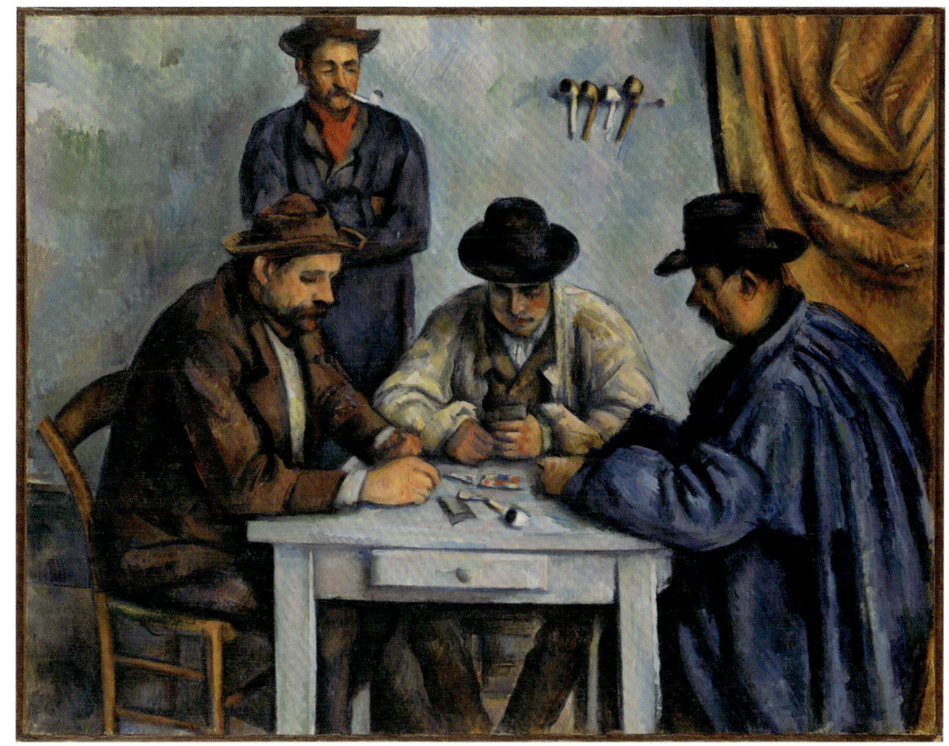

Another source for his sculptures in Perspex was a painting by Paul Cezanne, *The Card Players* (1890-91) which he admired at the Metropolitan Museum of Art with the curator Gary Tinterow in 2010, on his last visit to New York, for his second exhibition on the museum's sculpture garden on the roof. His interest deepened when the same painting became the subject of an exhibition at the Courtauld Gallery in 2011. As with his source sculptures, the fascination was not colour but composition.[7] Caro's response was *Sackbut* (2011-12) [pgs.70-71], in which he combined clear plastic with steel, rusted and waxed. This was the first of his new series of Perspex sculptures. Caro had begun with two crushed steel forms that had proved surplus to his *Chapel of Light* commission in the Church of Saint-Jean-Baptiste in Bourbourg, near Calais. At first he divided them with a sheet of glass but it proved unwieldy and easily chipped. Pat suggested substituting the glass with a sheet of Perspex, which can still be damaged by scuffing and scratching but such marks can at least be buffed and polished away. As a vertical divider the sheet of Perspex performed just like glass in the way it reflects the two sides of the game of cards. However, at first Caro rejected the Perspex as 'fake glass.' Pat recalls, 'Tony didn't like it being invisible, he had a big problem with that, so we sanded the edges to give them a frosted appearance, to make it look more solid'. Gradually he realised that, as a material, Perspex had advanced technologically and now had greater potential than when he used it for *Duccio Variations*. To make that sculpture seem 'more real' Caro found he had to set it on a grey floor.

For his next work, *Autumn Rhapsody* (2011-12) [pgs. 23-25], Caro explored the addition of colour to Perspex, and this proved challenging. Perspex is made clear and then coloured by applying a veneer of thinner sheets of coloured material to one side, coating a 20mm clear sheet with a sheet of colour between 3 and 5mm thick, depending on the depth of colour he required. No veneer is needed for the edges for they seem to take on the colour of the sides. The effect can seem magical, especially if one peers deep inside the length of a sheet lined with colour, where the reflected space seems to open up inside, as if one is swimming beneath the surface of a river. However, when the sheets are chamfered (cut not square but at an oblique angle) to meet the steel sculpture, then the edges of Perspex behave quite differently. Like strips of shining mirrors, they take on a linear quality, emphasizing their geometry, like drawing in the air. As Pat recalls, 'the edges became the drawing of the piece as the rest fades away.' To achieve such precision sheets of plywood were first used and then measured as templates. The Perspex components had to be made and assembled by a specialist supplier of shop signs and window displays working to Computer Assisted Drawings by one of Caro's studio assistants, Olivia Bax. Sheila Girling would join the team to discuss the choice of colour for the Perspex before the plywood template was removed. A month or two could pass before the Perspex components would return ready to replace the templates, by which time Caro's impatience would turn into renewed enthusiasm as he returned to challenges with fresh eyes.

The choice of colour for the Perspex could not be changed once ordered. Despite Caro wearing a chained set of samples around the studio, like a hippie's necklace, the samples proved too small to indicate their true colour as sheets. For *Autumn Rhapsody* the pristine new citrus yellow Perspex made the painted steel look dirty. To get the colour right Caro had the steel repainted. It took sixteen attempts. Through the Perspex and in its cast shadow the blue-grey steel looked green. Olivia Bax recalls that 'it went from a grey undercoat through green, yellow, whites and greys. Each day would end with it solved but then next morning Tony would see it afresh and I had to paint it again.' This was partly because of the way coloured Perspex behaves. Unlike painted or intrinsic colour Perspex overflows, for it casts coloured shadows and invites the viewer to look through it, so seeing parts of the sculpture veiled by its colour. In this way Perspex is more painterly than paint, and closer to glazes. Caro soon came to appreciate these qualities; he enjoyed experimenting with the transmission of light through layering and abutting sheets of coloured Perspex and soon learned how to master his new medium.

Alpine (2011-12) [pgs. 42-43] came more quickly, the final colour of choice being simply the initial grey undercoat. The visual effect of the straight Perspex sheets against the crumpled painted steel is a reversal of what one might expect, for the steel looks soft by comparison, like a tissue or snow. For *Terminus* (2013) [pgs. 28-29] the choice of a sheet of 'frosted raspberry red' Perspex came from the residual colour of the scrap steel (a jib off an old crane). Caro so liked the red of the sheet once it arrived that, as another assistant, Neil Ayling recalled, 'He had me recreate the effect of the original distressed colour, to repeat it in a colour composition, like faux decoration, to unify it all. After the sheet of coloured Perspex arrived he wanted the surface of the steel reworked, to put its lost colour back in, in a way that looked accidental.'

In *Terminus* the extra touches of red help to unify the piece, for warm colour also comes from two railway sleepers joined together, cantilevered to appear floating over the Perspex, despite their obvious weight. This interest in the intrinsic colour and surface finish of salvaged materials alongside sheets of new Perspex is also evident in *Sundown* (2013) [pgs. 64-65]. The core ingredient was a former sand hopper, inverted, with other scrap steel

Anthony Caro, figure drawings
(with corrections by Henry Moore)
1951-52, Mixed media on vellum
approx. 22 x 15 inches (55.8 x 38.1 cm)

patched in. Neil Ayling recalls how he was guided by Caro to unify the steel collage visually, but not by giving it a single coat of paint: 'He got me to extend all the old scars, like the grinding marks and rust stains. He knew precisely where he wanted a rust line to finish, so I used a chemical primer or acrylics to extend a line. He used to say: 'Extend the grey' and 'Can you fudge it?' Painting was definitely a tool for unifying, layering and adding depth.'

As Caro became more familiar with Perspex he became more experimental. As with his approach to steel, he sought out scrapped, rejected components and recycled them. In *Blue Moon* (2013) [pgs. 58-59], the last of the Perspex series, he began not with steel and a plywood template, but with the Perspex itself, after salvaging a dome that another customer had rejected at the Perspex factory. Knowing by now how Perspex would behave, he set the dome beneath a sheet of plywood that was carefully 'slumped' to form a sweeping downward plane. The plywood became the precise template for a slumped sheet of Perspex. Caro liked the resemblance to a large lens and after careful deliberations he decided that the dome should be painted blue, on the underside only. Neil painted it in acrylic, each brush stroke in the same direction, giving a deliberate streaky effect when seen from the upper side.

Caro's attention to the painterly finish may seem surprising, given the customary accounts of how 'Caro's wife often painted the finished works in bright household colours'[8] after the sculptural part of making sculpture was over. But Caro always decided the colour in the end and his interest went beyond the choice of single colours. His exploration of subtler effects, of modulated surface finishes, may derive from his training under Henry Moore for whom, as part of his duties, he learnt the art of creating patination on bronzes.

In the second half of this two-venue exhibition the theme is line. Caro's conviction that the series of drawings of a man and bull still 'stood up' after fifty years in storage is shared by any viewer today. Now shown in New York for the first time, these drawings confirm that Caro valued the approach of working in series five or so years before he

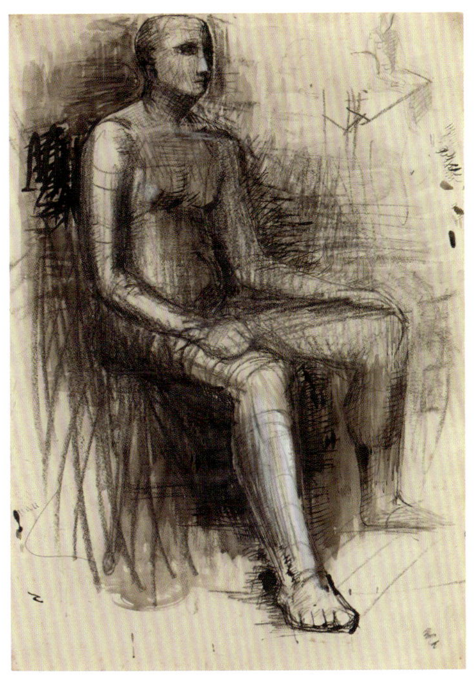
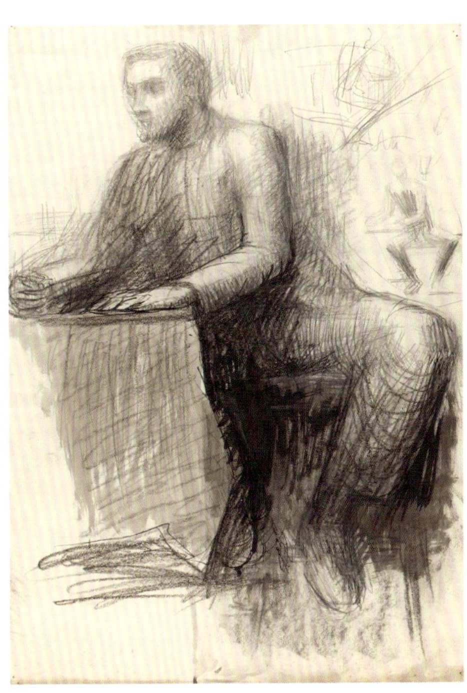
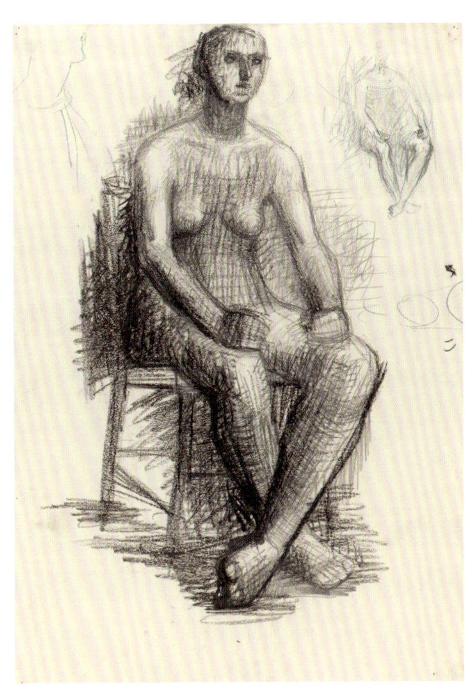
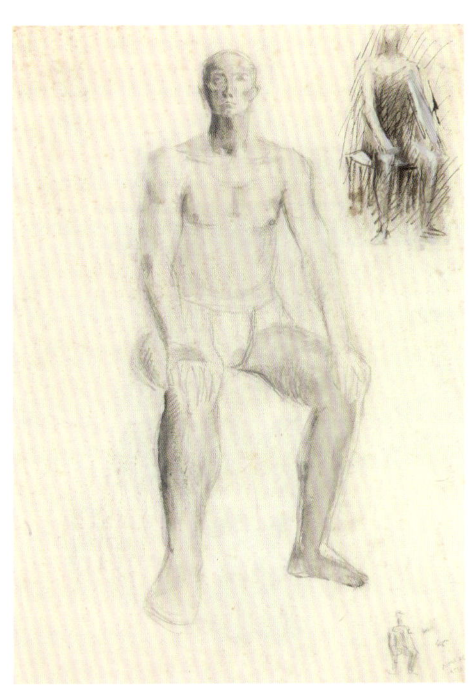

first met Kenneth Noland and David Smith in 1959. For an artist trained in the life class of the Royal Academy they could not be more different than the drawings he showed to Henry Moore, who then annotated them to help Caro see as a sculptor.[9]

Like the coloured drawings they are of course closer to Picasso and suggest an artist seeking to reinvent his whole approach and at the same time expressing his frustration. The crawling man seems to be screaming in pain, (e.g. *Figure,* 1955/56 [pg. 57]), perhaps even metamorphosing into the bull that belongs to the same group of drawings, while caged in by the edges of each sheet of paper.

When he made these drawings Caro had yet to meet Greenberg in London or to follow his advice and visit New York. More Anglo-French than Anglo-American in outlook, he shared the Existentialist concerns of artists looking to Paris and sought, as he said, to try to express what it felt like to be inside a body. The first work by Caro to enter a public collection was *Woman Waking Up* (1955) which the Tate Gallery purchased on the recommendation of

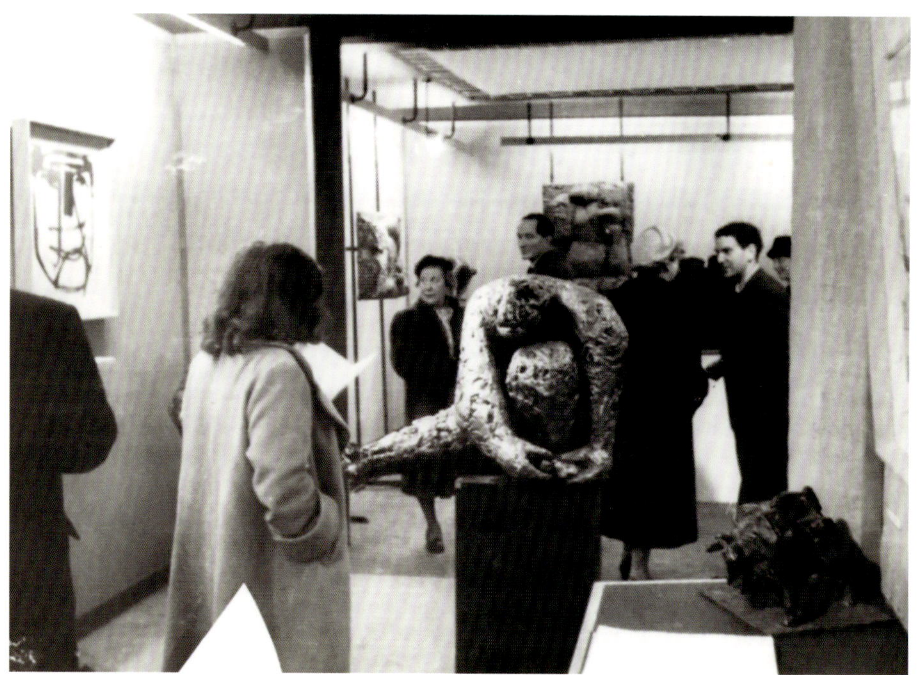

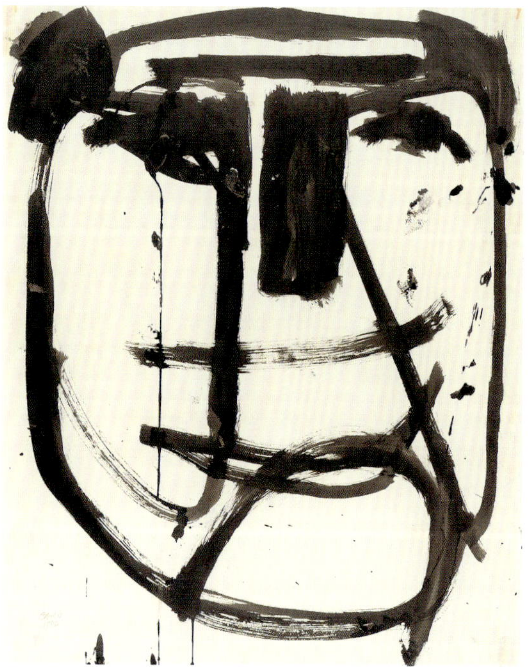

Far left: First U.K. one man show at Gimpels Fils Gallery, 1957

Left: *Head*
1956, Brush and ink
23 ⅜ x 18 ⅛ inches 0(59.5 x 46 cm)
Victoria and Albert Museum, London

Henry Moore in 1959. The next year, the second work by Caro to enter a public collection was a brush and ink drawing, signed and dated 1956, purchased by the Victoria and Albert Museum in 1960. Its importance to Caro is clear from a photograph of Caro receiving guests at his first one-man exhibition in Britain, at Gimpel Fils Gallery in 1957, where the same drawing can be seen on the left. Caro had seen works by Willem de Kooning and Jackson Pollock in exhibitions at London's Institute of Contemporary Art in 1953. The speed of his laden brush and acceptance of its drips and splashes across this drawing reflects his admiration for the vitality of their art.[10]

The energy and fluency of his drawings suggest a sense of release from the practical constraints of working as a sculptor. Caro's natural diligence is evident otherwise from the neat italic script of his correspondence with Noland, Greenberg, Fried, Olitski and other Americans after his return in 1960. There are also the precise drawings he made to record every sculpture, with its dimensions, title and date, as soon as it was finished, as part of his studio records. Caro's admiration for Matisse influenced the bright palette he used for his painted sculptures but also his fluent figure drawings when he returned to the life model in 1983. A large life drawing by David Smith always hung above his desk in his studio office as a daily challenge. As Smith said in a lecture in 1955: 'drawings remain the life force of the artist. Especially is this true for the sculptor, who, of necessity, works in media slow to take realization.'[11]

The decision to show these drawings with sculptures in the Madison Avenue gallery came from the wish to demonstrate the consistency of Caro's vision, the directing force and energy within the sculptures on view. At the risk of oversimplification, Caro uses line in at least three ways in his sculptures: defining, directing and digressing. In the drawings the edge of the paper seems to act as a container, giving some sense of security to the baby with its ball (e.g. *Baby With a Ball,* 1954 [pg. 21]), and, by contrast, a cage-like constraint to the crawling man. In a similar way Caro uses the silhouettes of these sculptures and their defining outer contours. Inside, he animates with lines that go in different directions, taking their own paths to set rhythms running, rectilinear and architectonic in *Honey Suckle*, spiraling fast in *Sunlit* [pg. 35], staccato in *No Talking* [pg. 61] and fluent as a stream in *Table Piece CLIX* [pg. 49]. The third use of line is the element of surprise, when a line digresses from the prevailing rhythm, setting off for a walk on its own like a free doodle. Caro's drawings from the 1950s were neither preliminary sketches for sculptures nor were they imaginary sculptures but these exploratory exercises on newsprint were carefully preserved. They now provide a reminder of the thrill of the creative process when free from the practicalities of construction. Fortunately Caro soon established the studio and team he needed to keep up with his imagination, and the results were prolific.

End Notes

1 For the *Duccio* series see Ian Barker, *Anthony Caro. Quest for the New Sculpture* (Kunzelsau, Swiridoff Verlag, 2004) p. 331. Caro's wife, Sheila Girling, had used Perspex in 1987 at the Triangle Workshop.

2 Caro to Diana Eichler, quoted in Barker, 2004, pp 21-22. Gabo and Pevsner published their *Realistic Manifesto* in 1920 which launched abstract art as the form for the age, using new materials.

3 Bryan Robertson, *Colour Sculptures: Britain in the Sixties* (London, Waddington Galleries, 1999) cat. 9. See also Philip King, Tim Scott and William Turnbull, 'Colour in Sculpture. Statements', *Studio International*, vol. 177, no. 907 (January 1969) pp. 21-24.

4 Quoted in *Pool*, issue no. 1, unpaginated, (November 2011). Reference kindly provided by Olivia Bax.

5 Alastair Sooke, *Anthony Caro: The Last Sculptures*, (London, Annely Juda Fine Art, 2014) p. 9.

6 Julius Bryant and Rod Mengham, *Anthony Caro: The Figure* (London, Royal Society of British Sculptors, 2010).

7 Julius Bryant, *Anthony Caro: Figurative and Narrative Sculpture* (Farnham, Lund Humphries, 2009) pp. 29-30, 66-71.

8 Peter Fuller, 'London, Waddington Gallery & Knoedler Gallery. Anthony Caro.' *Burlington Magazine* volume 128 (December, 1986) pp. 916-18.

9 Julius Bryant and Martina Droth, *Caro Close Up,* (New Haven, Yale Center for British Art, 2012) pp. 83-91.

10 The drawing had been sold at Christie's 17 June 1960, lot 17. The Victoria and Albert Museum purchased it for 12 guineas, for the Circulation Department's School Loans collection (Circ. 290-1960).

11 Jorn Merkert, ed., *David Smith: Sculpture and Drawings*, (Munich, Prestel Verlag,1986) p. 155.

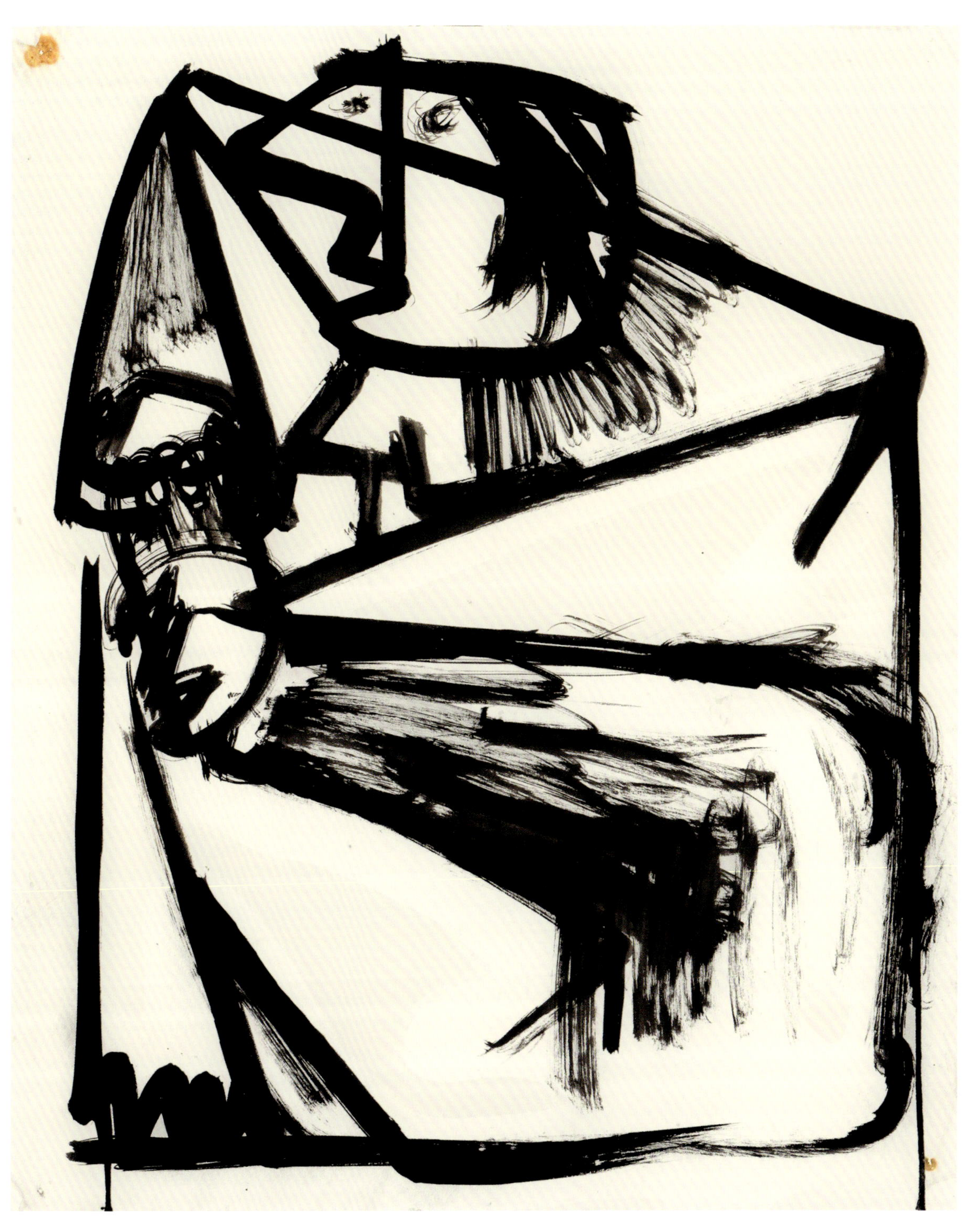

Baby With a Ball 1954

Autumn Rhapsody 2011/2012

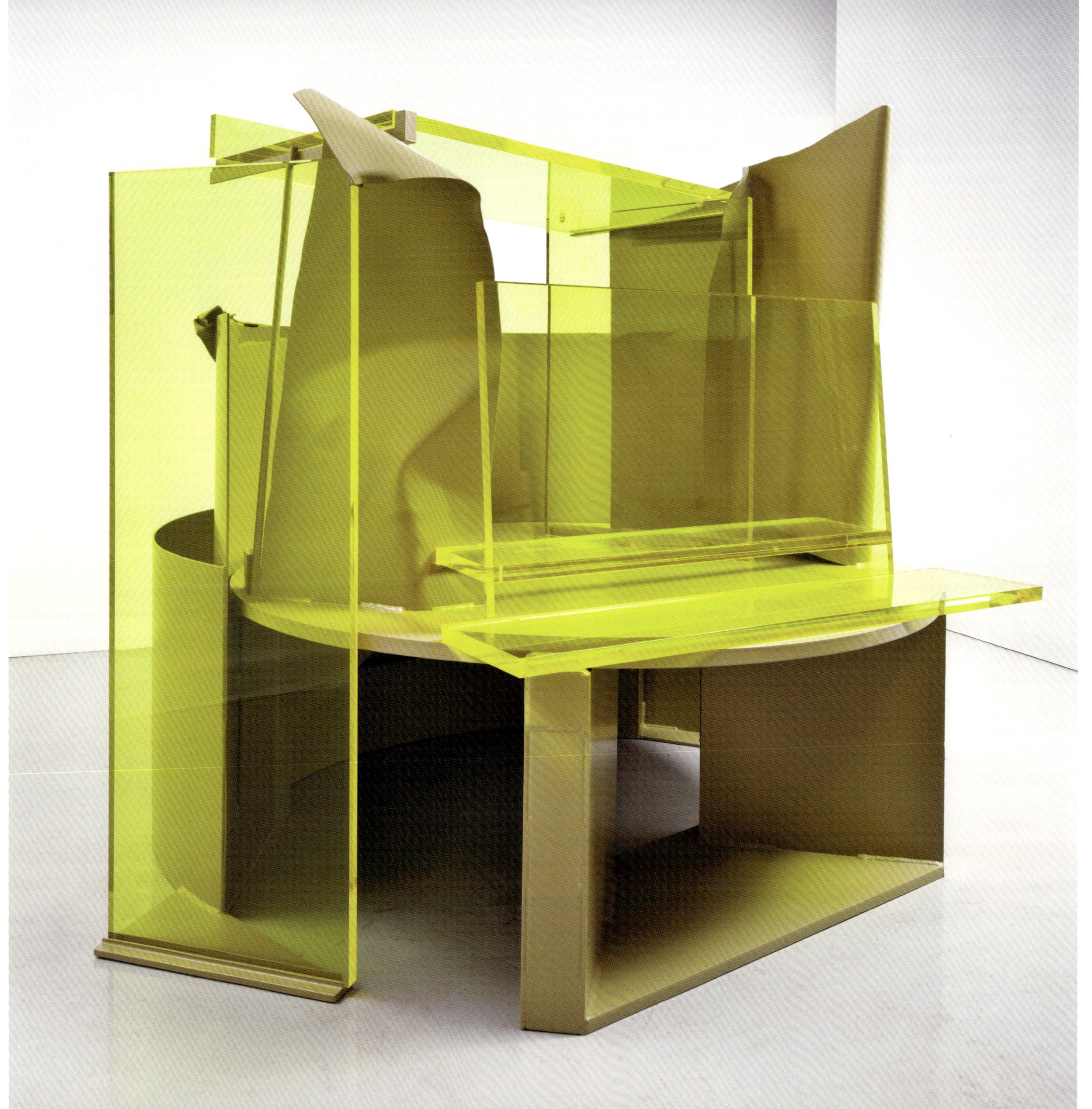

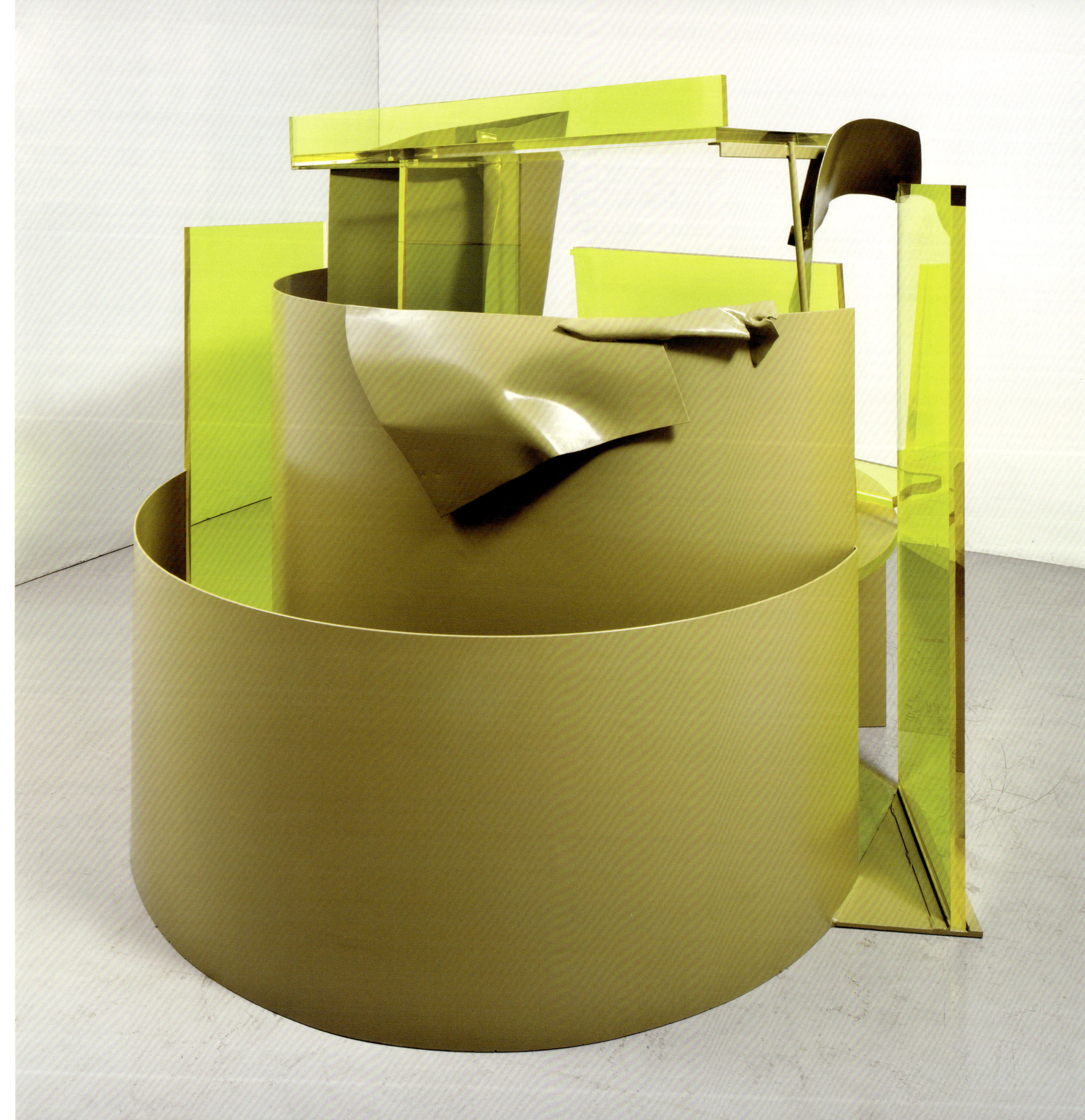

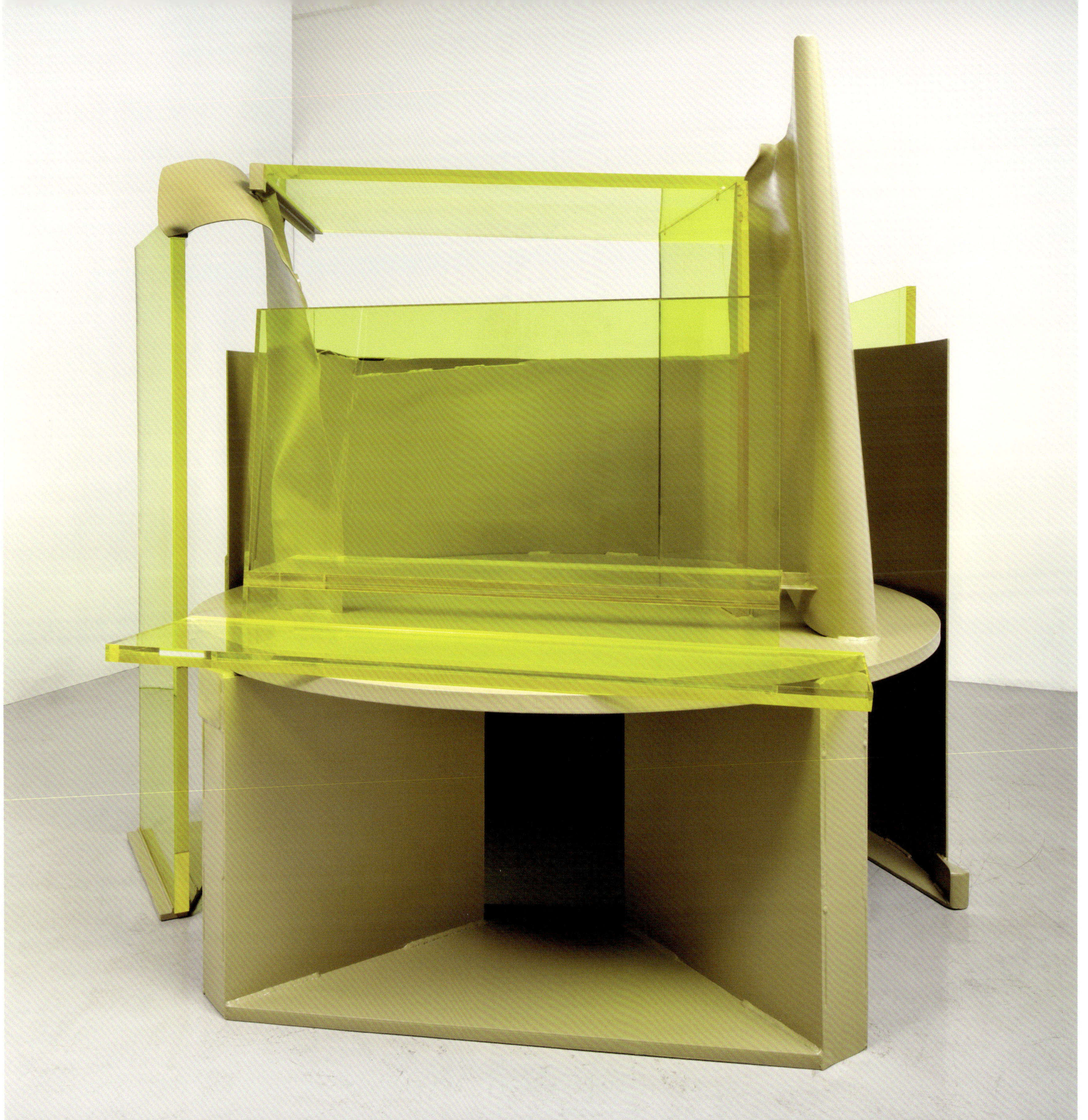

Figure 1955/1956

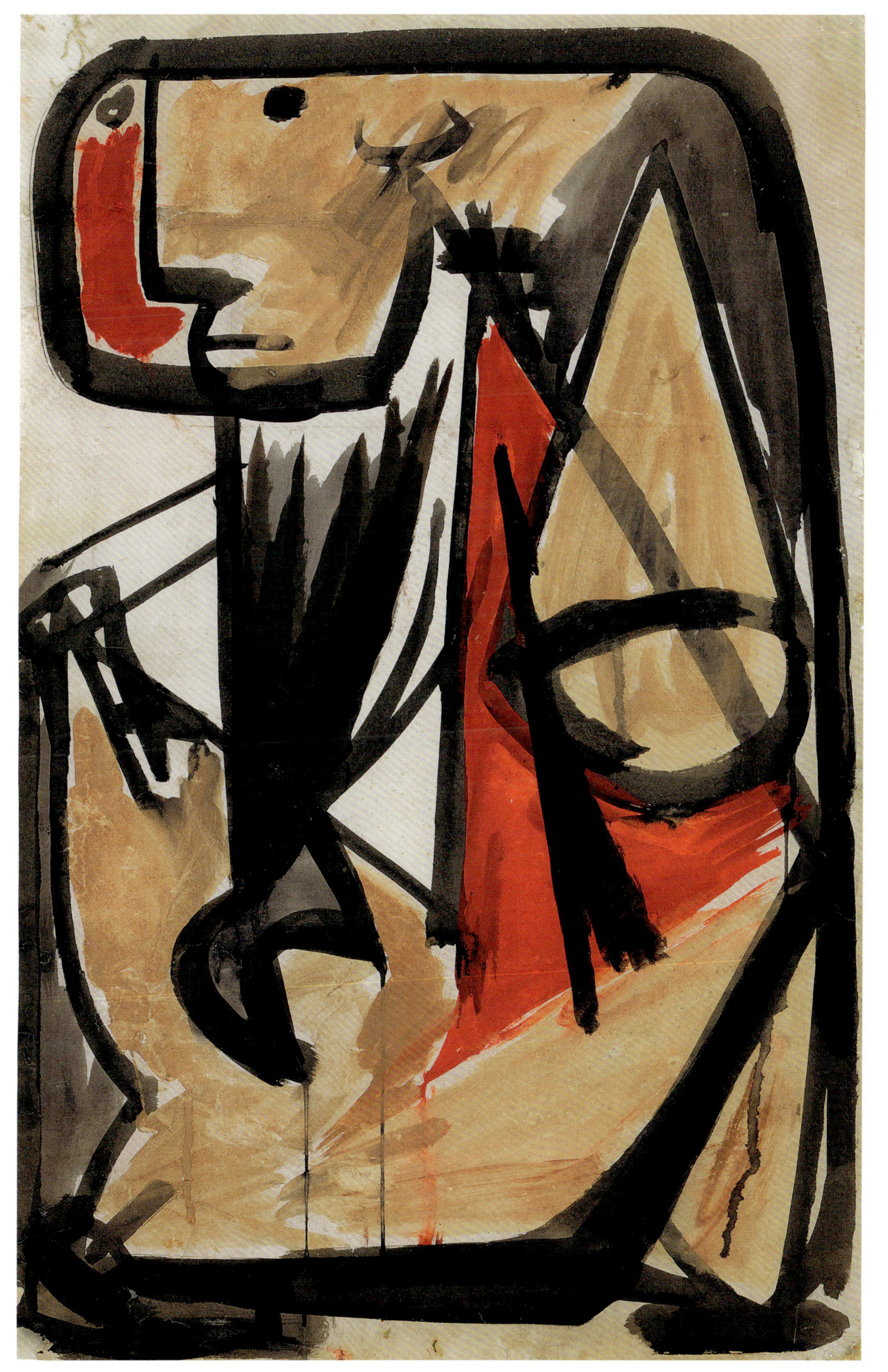

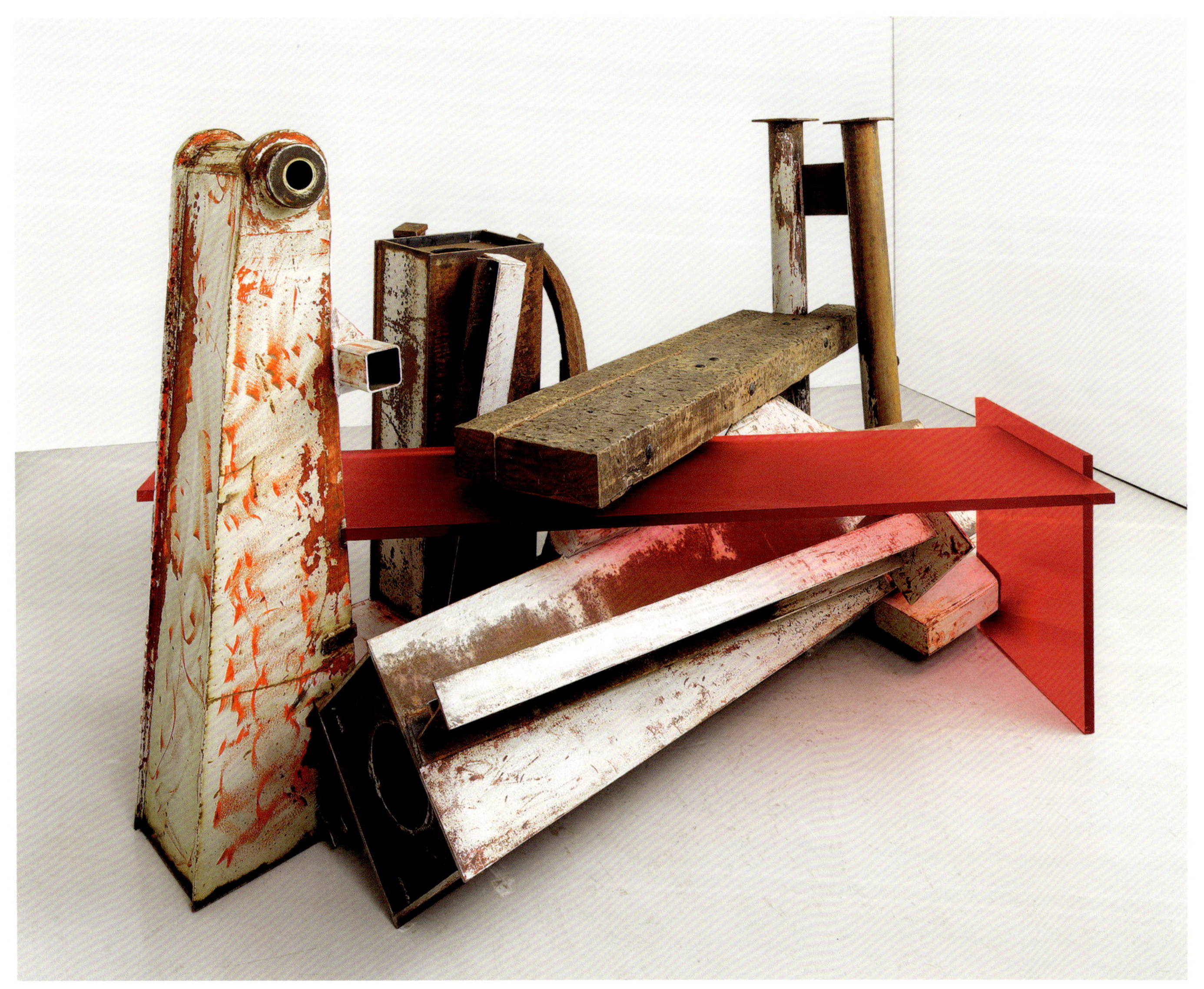

Terminus 2013

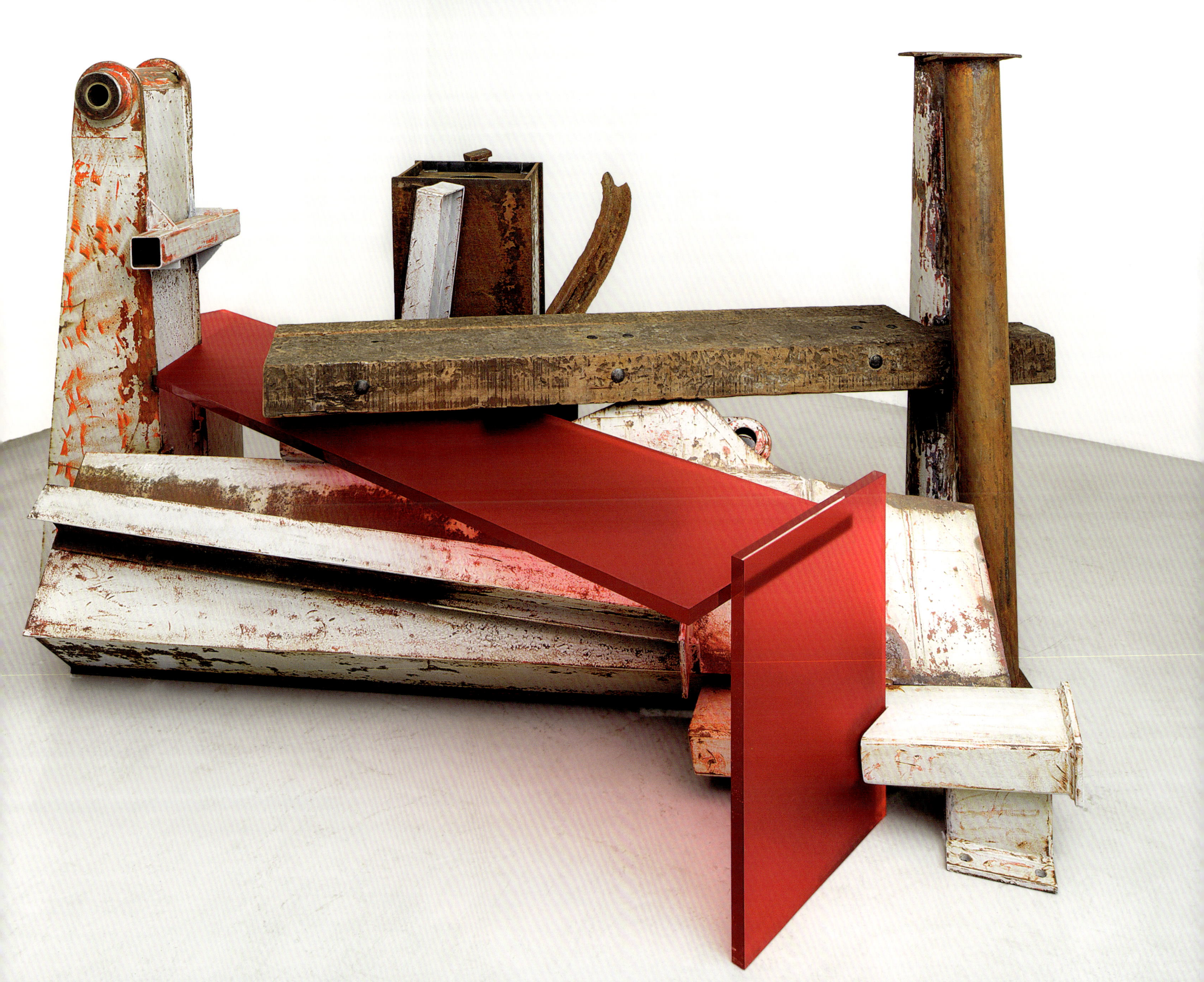

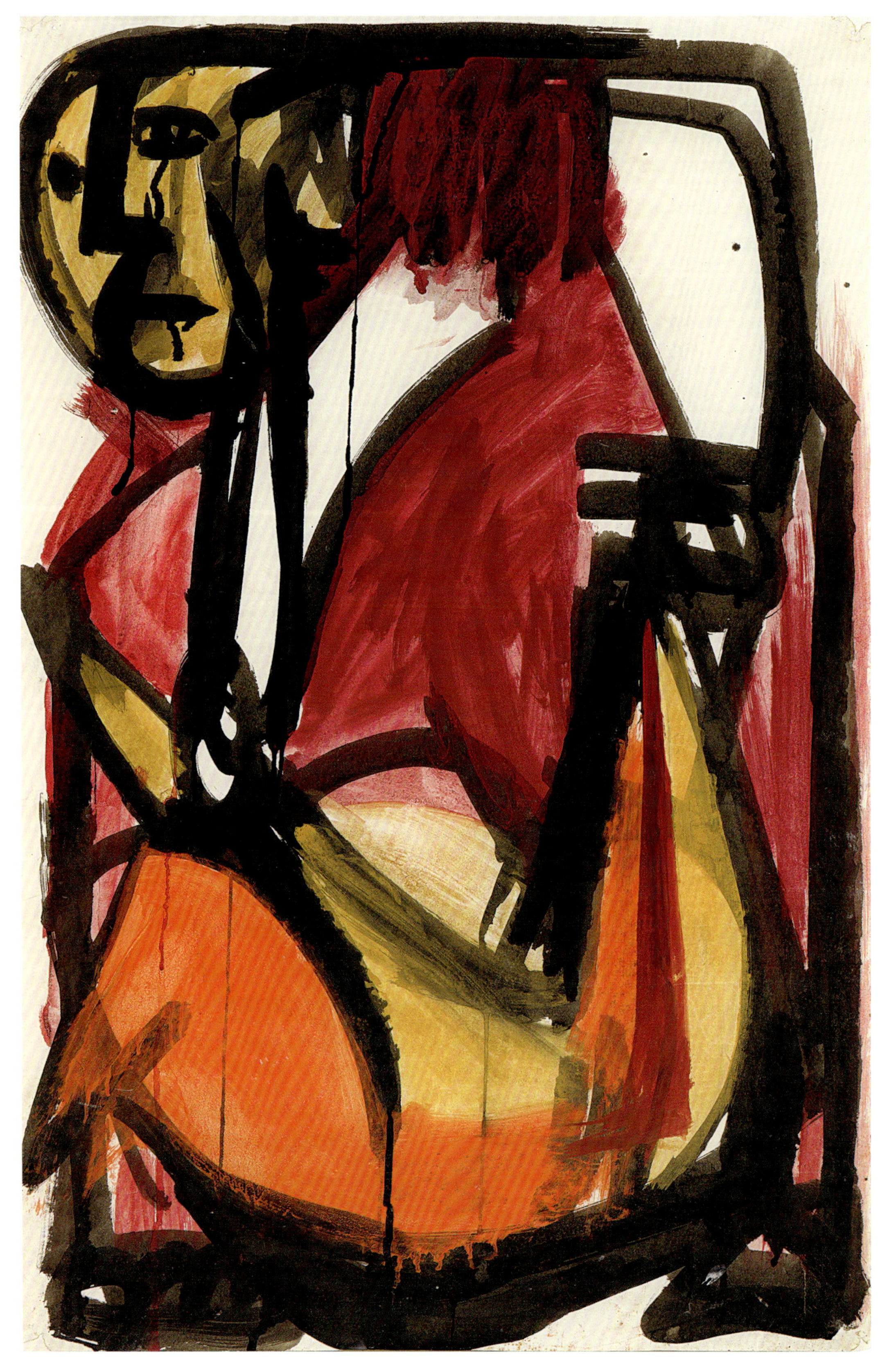

Figure 1955/1956

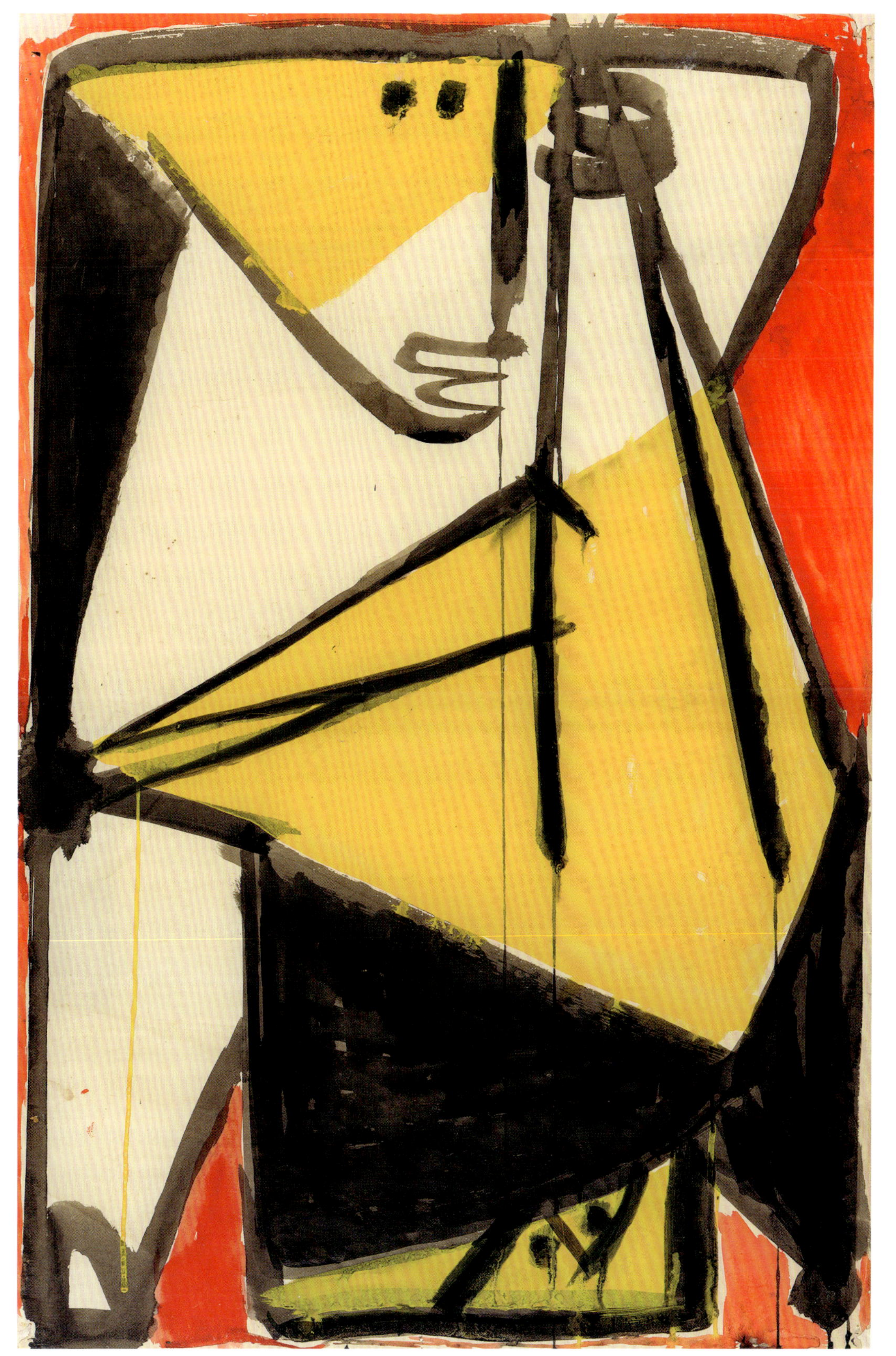

Warrior 1955/1956

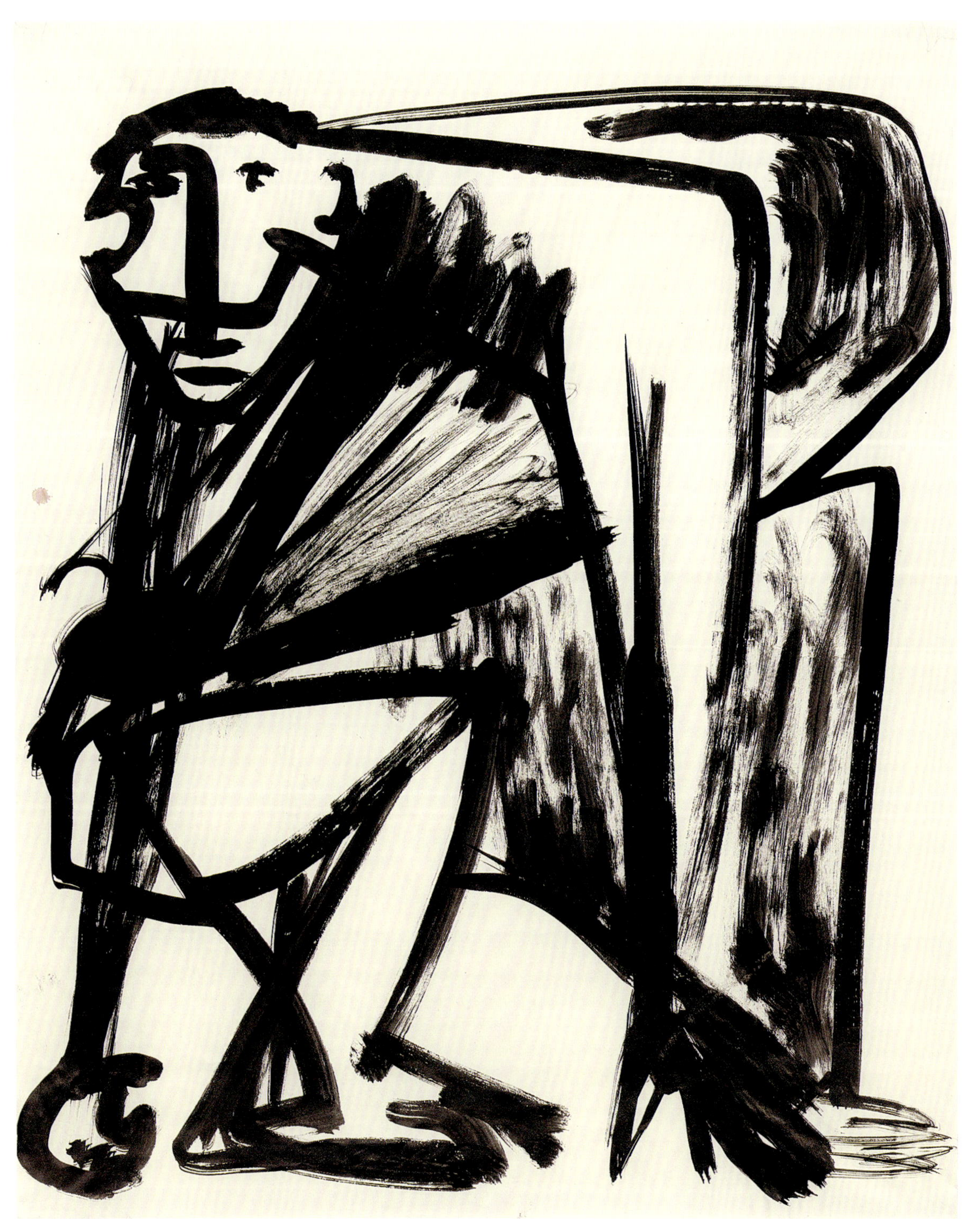

Seated Figure 1954

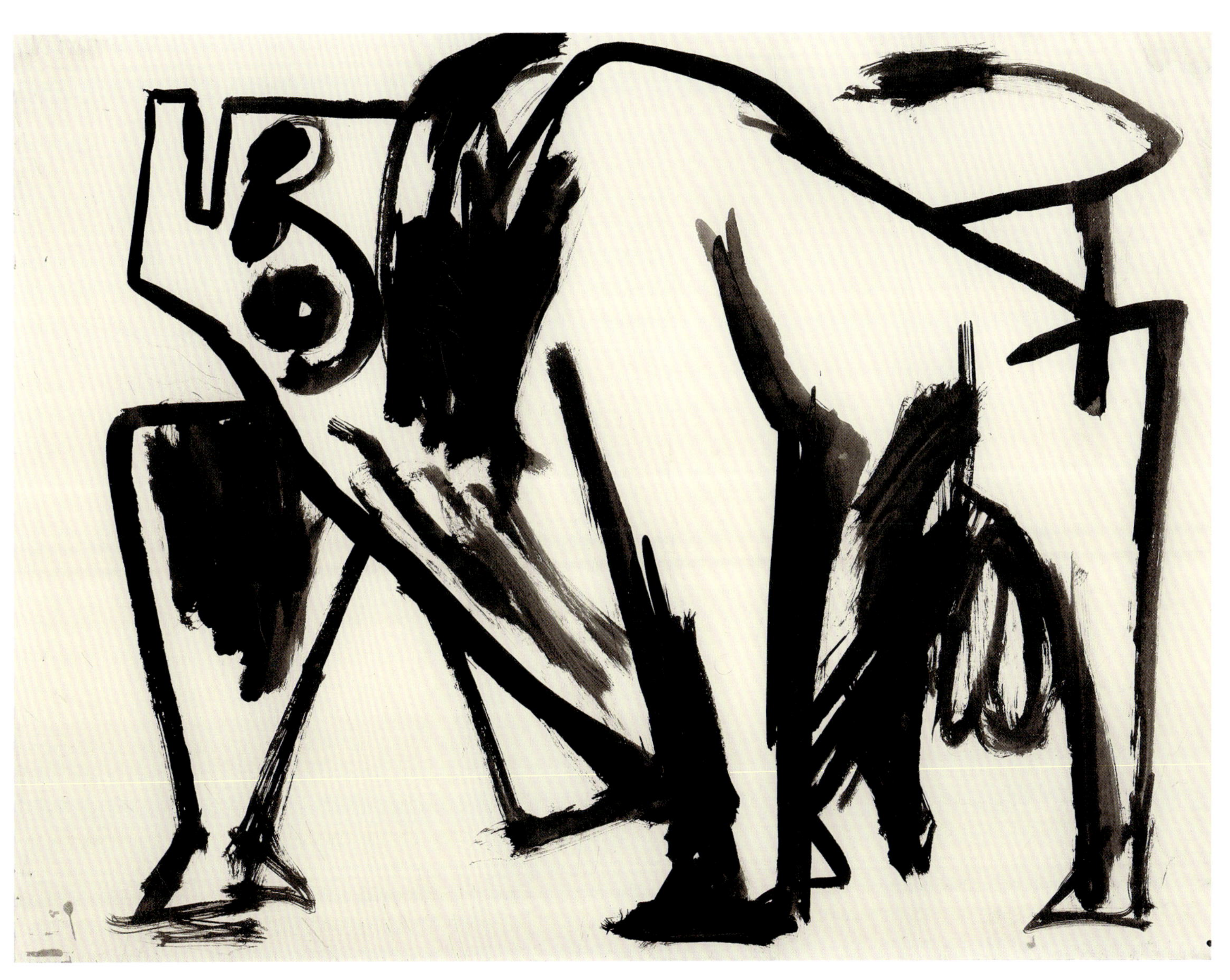

Bull 1954

Sunlit (Table Bronze) 1981/1982

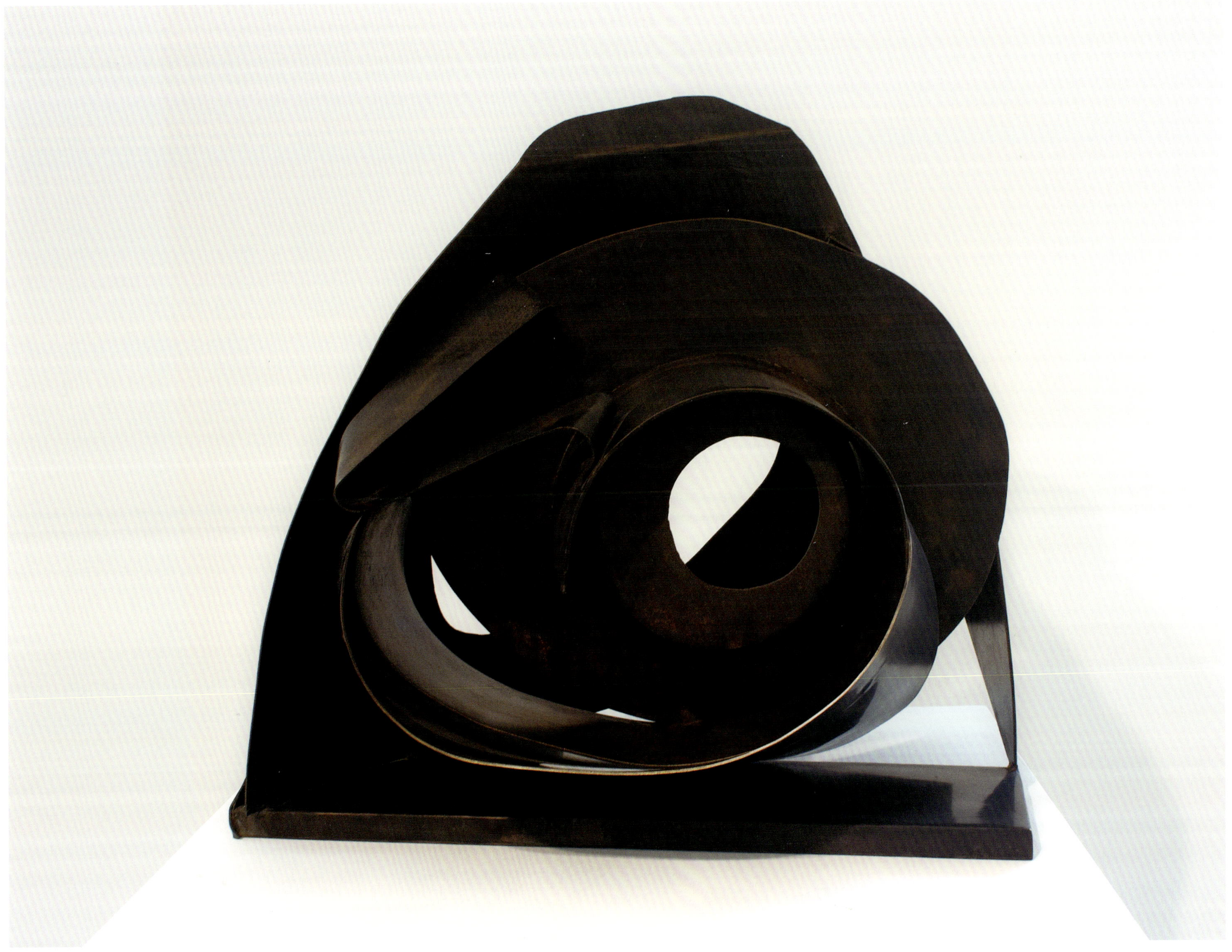

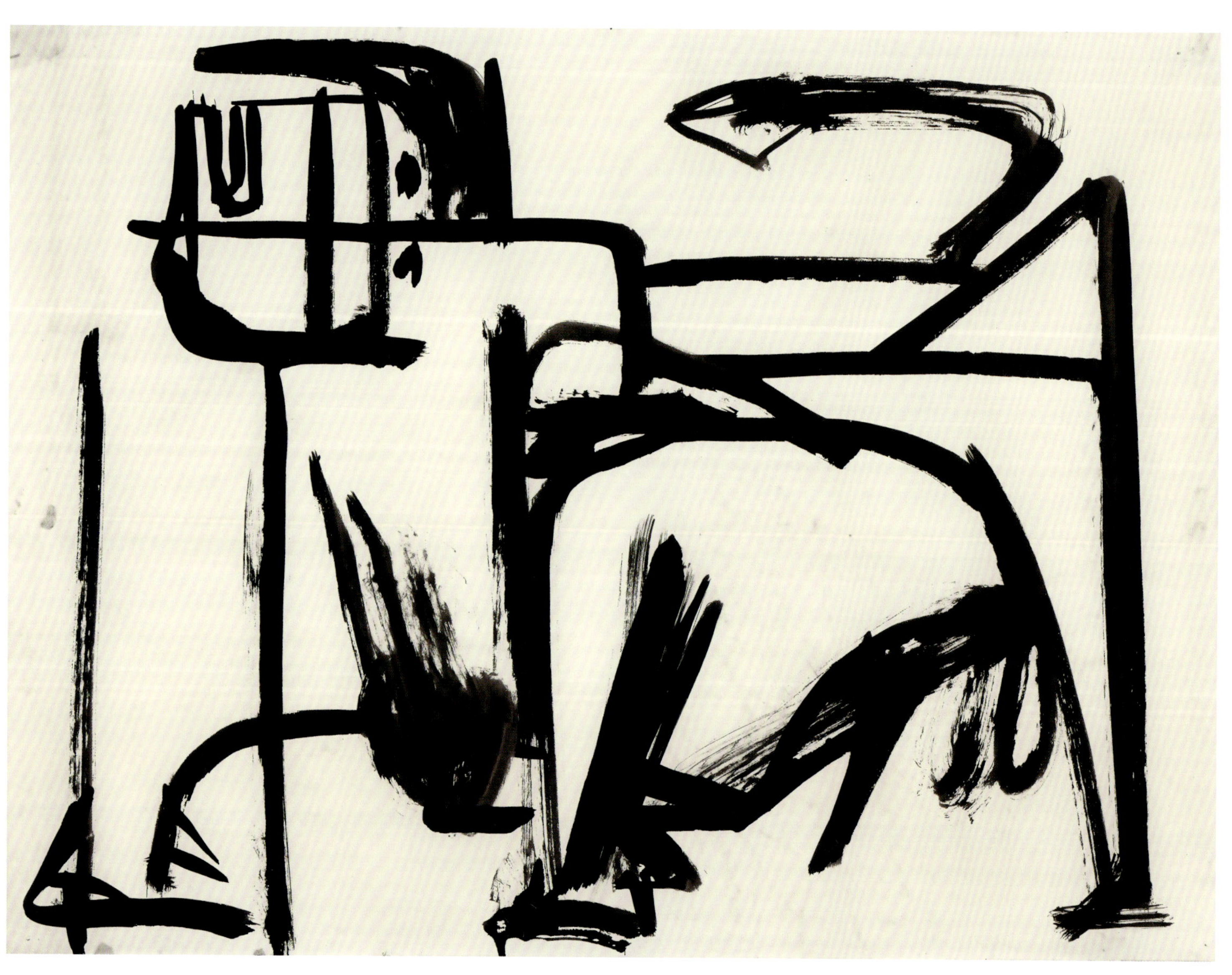

Bull 1954

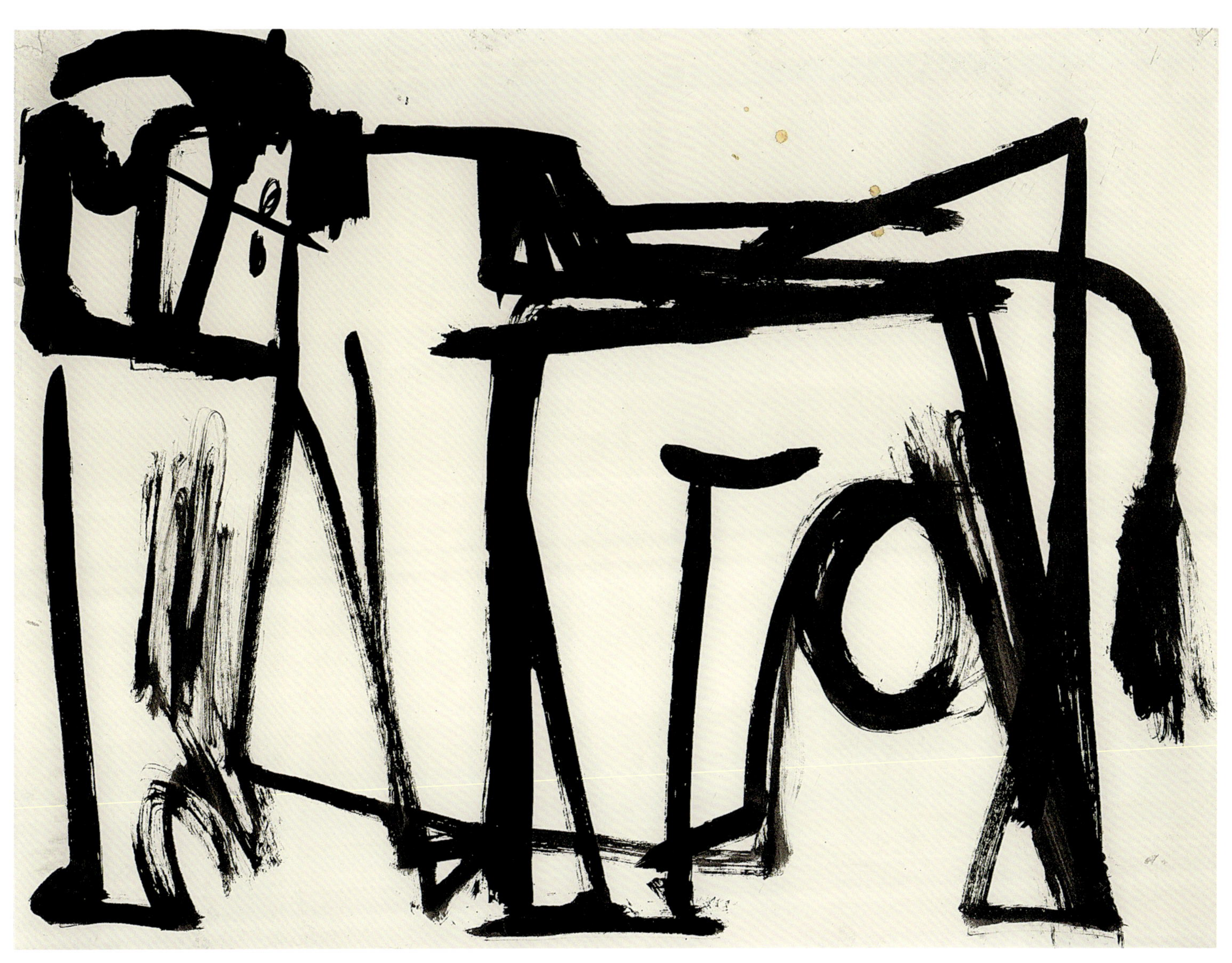

Bull 1954

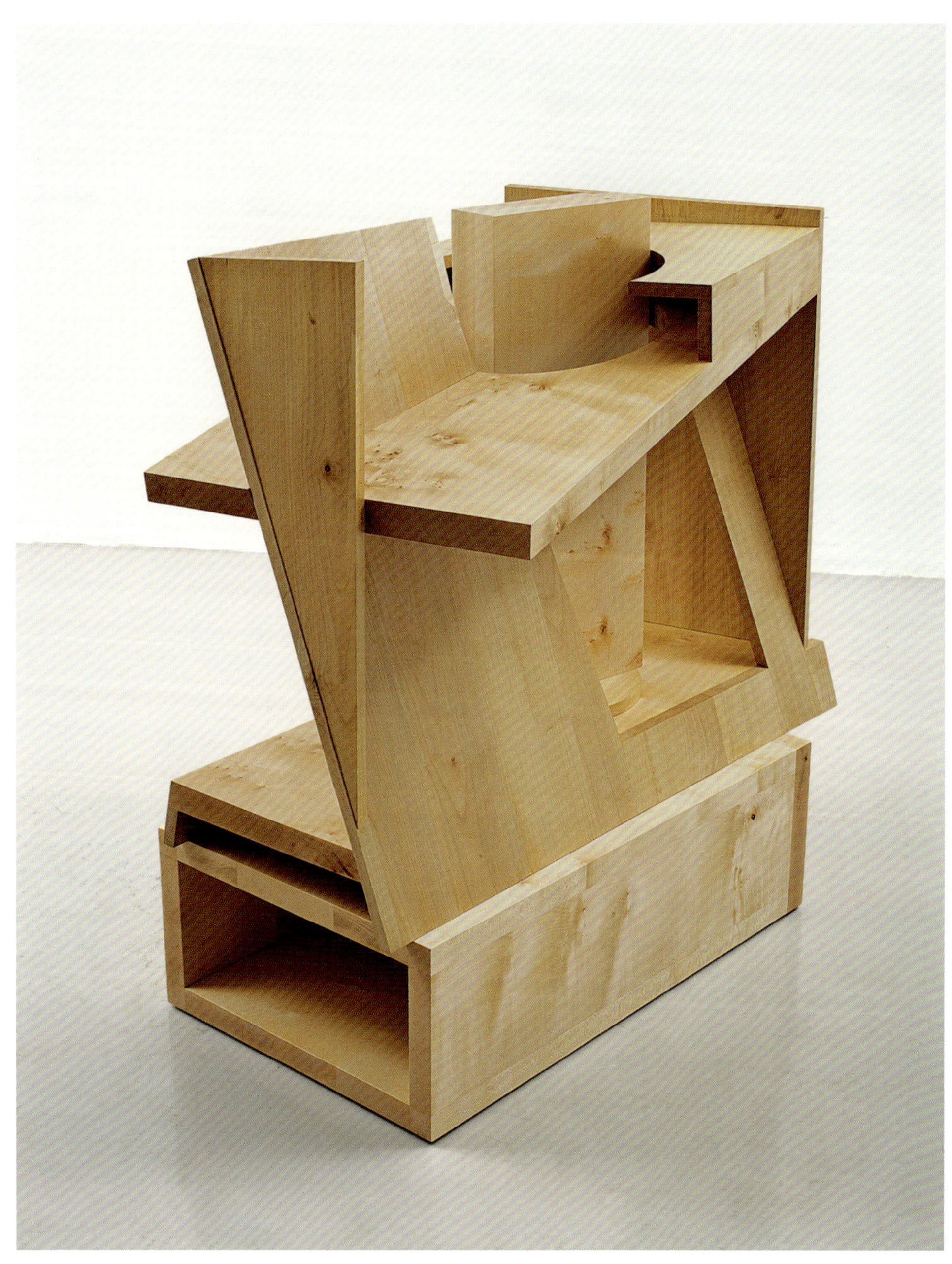

Honey Suckle 2011/2012

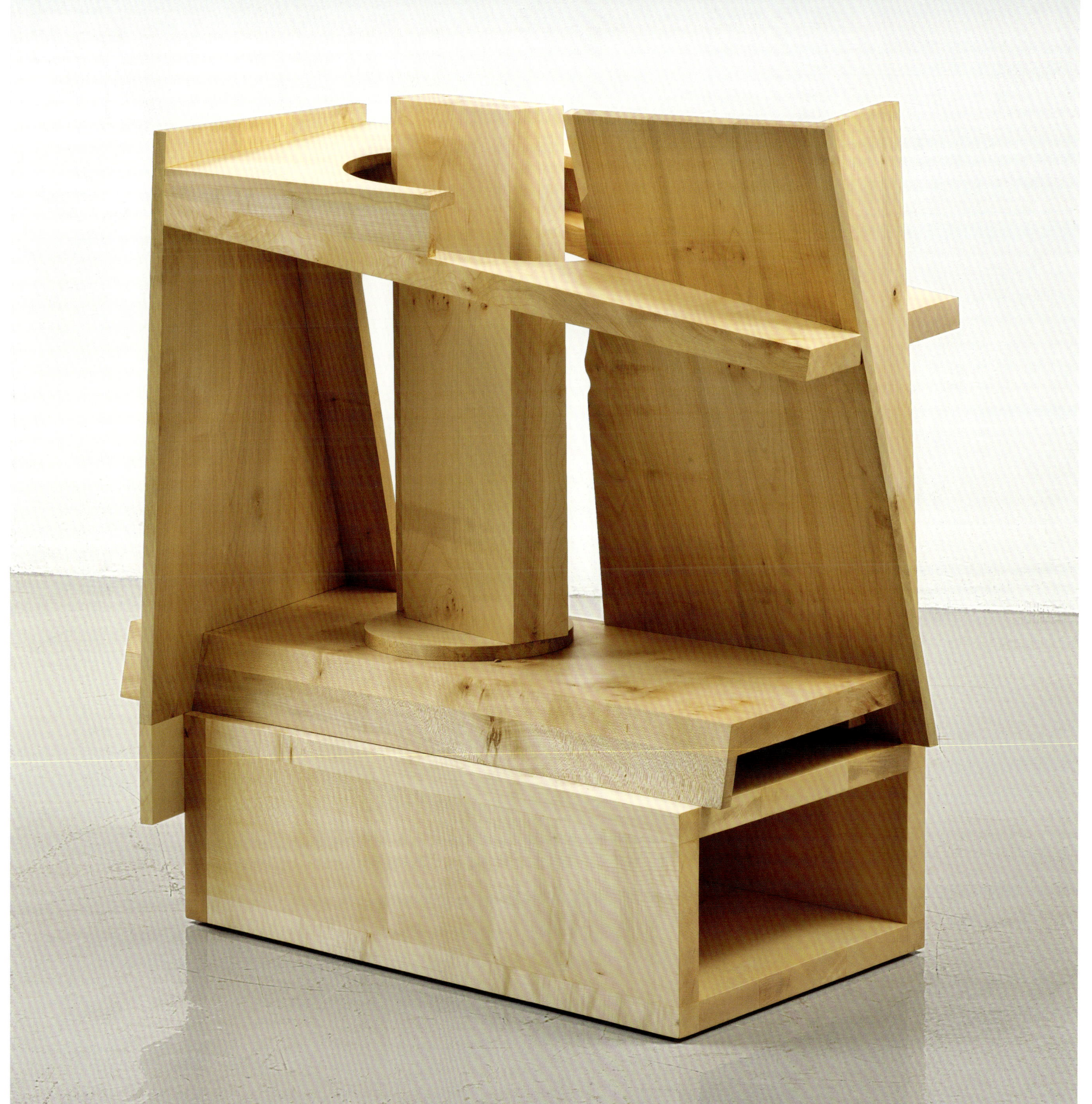

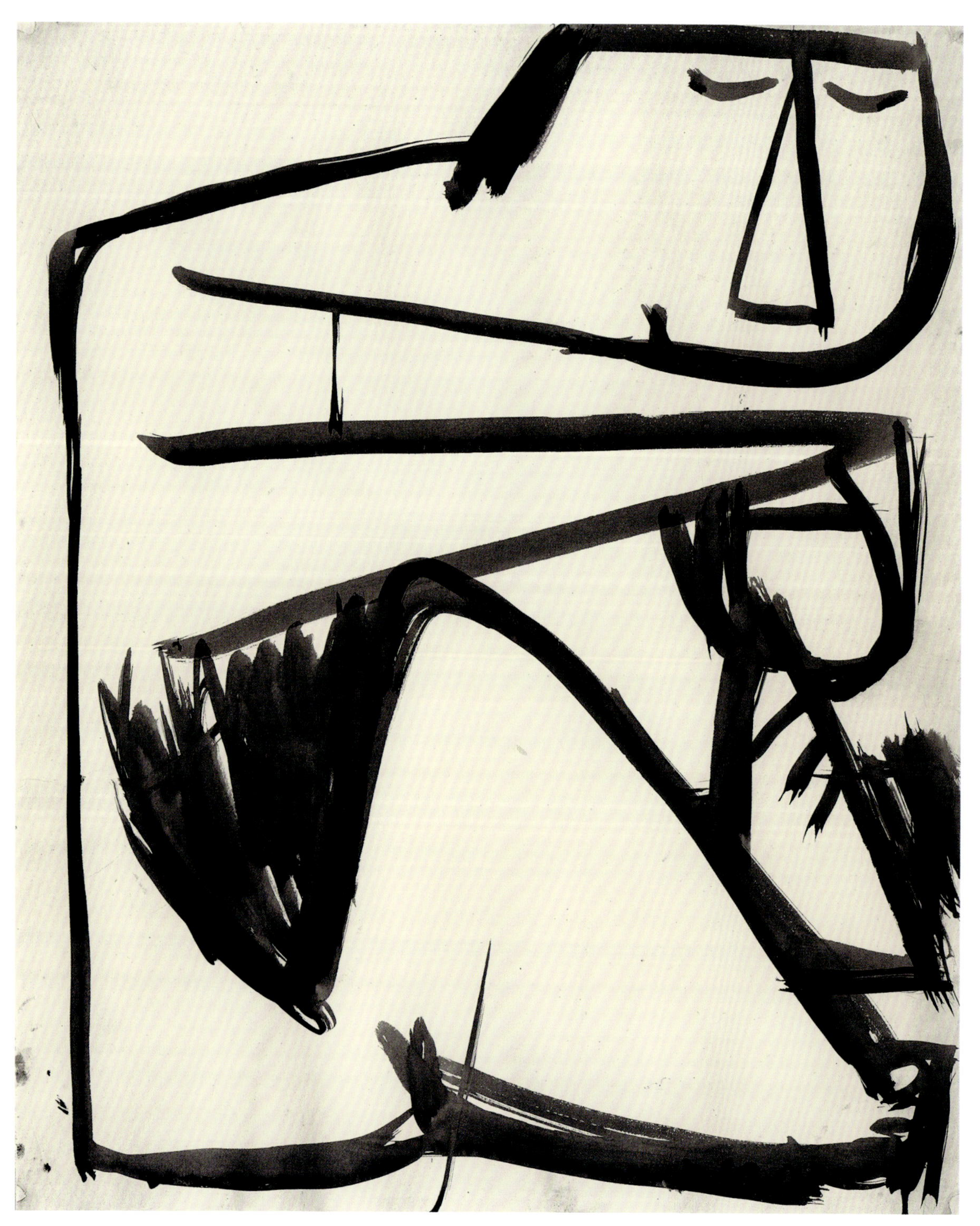

Baby With a Ball 1954

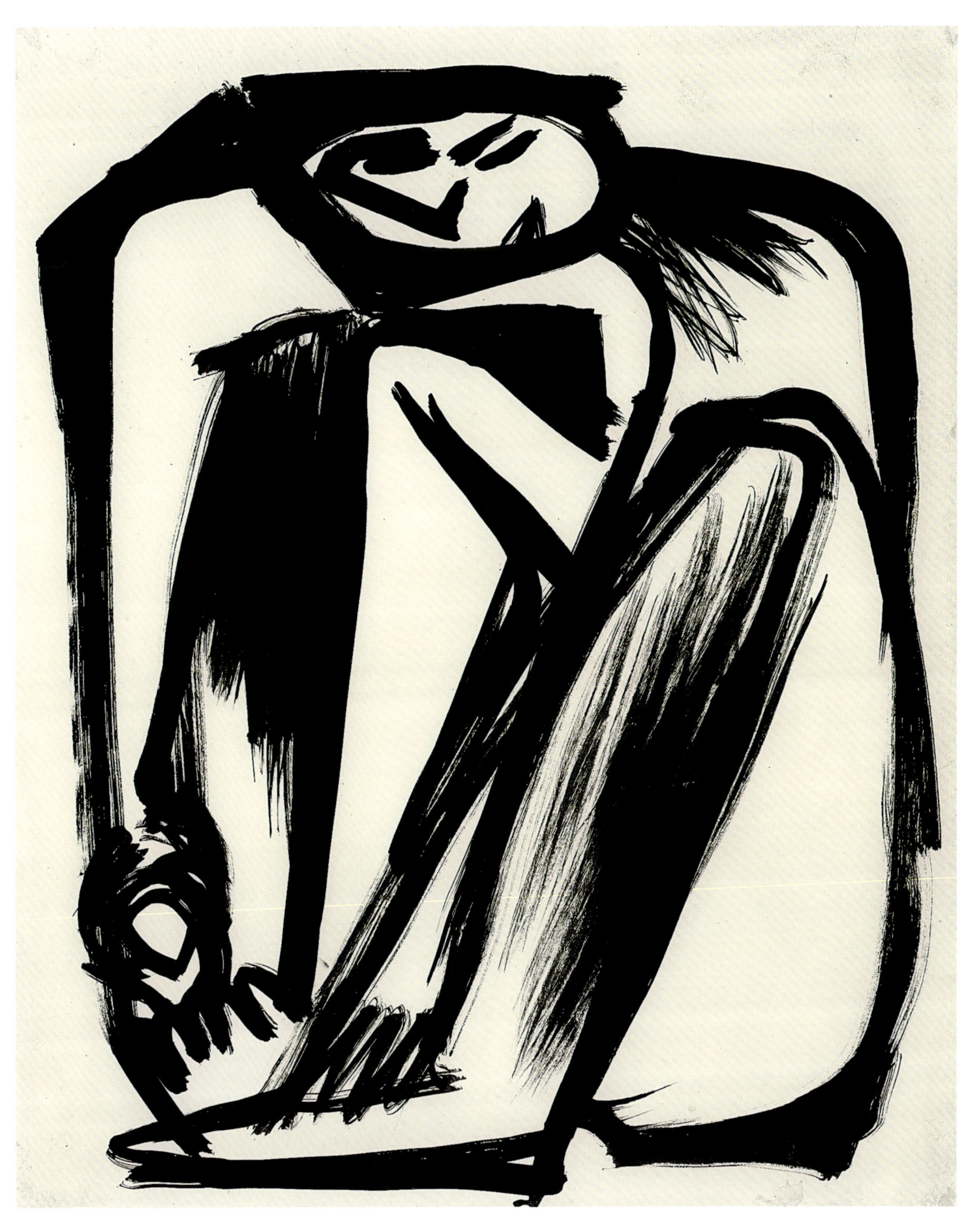

Baby With a Ball 1954

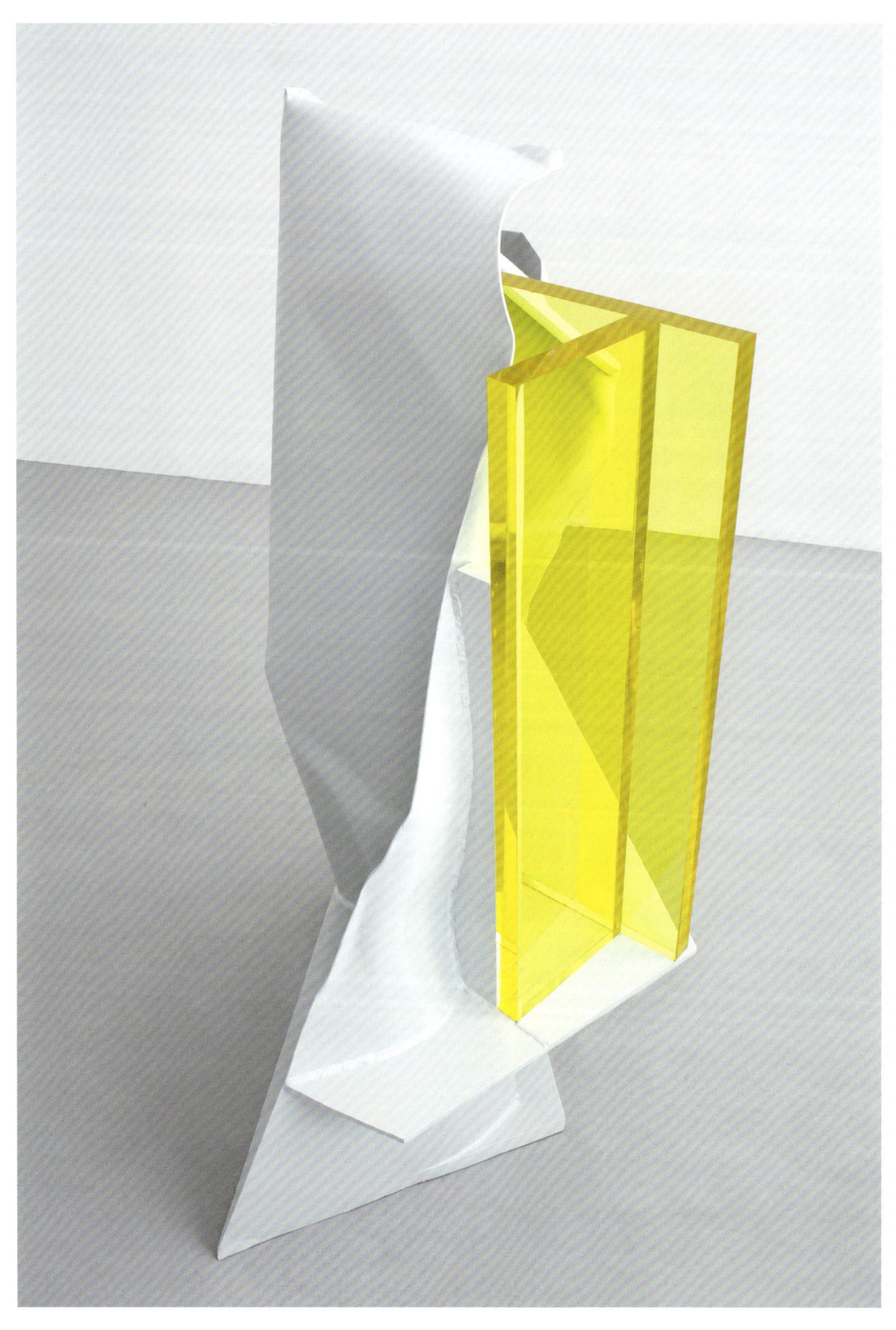

Alpine 2012

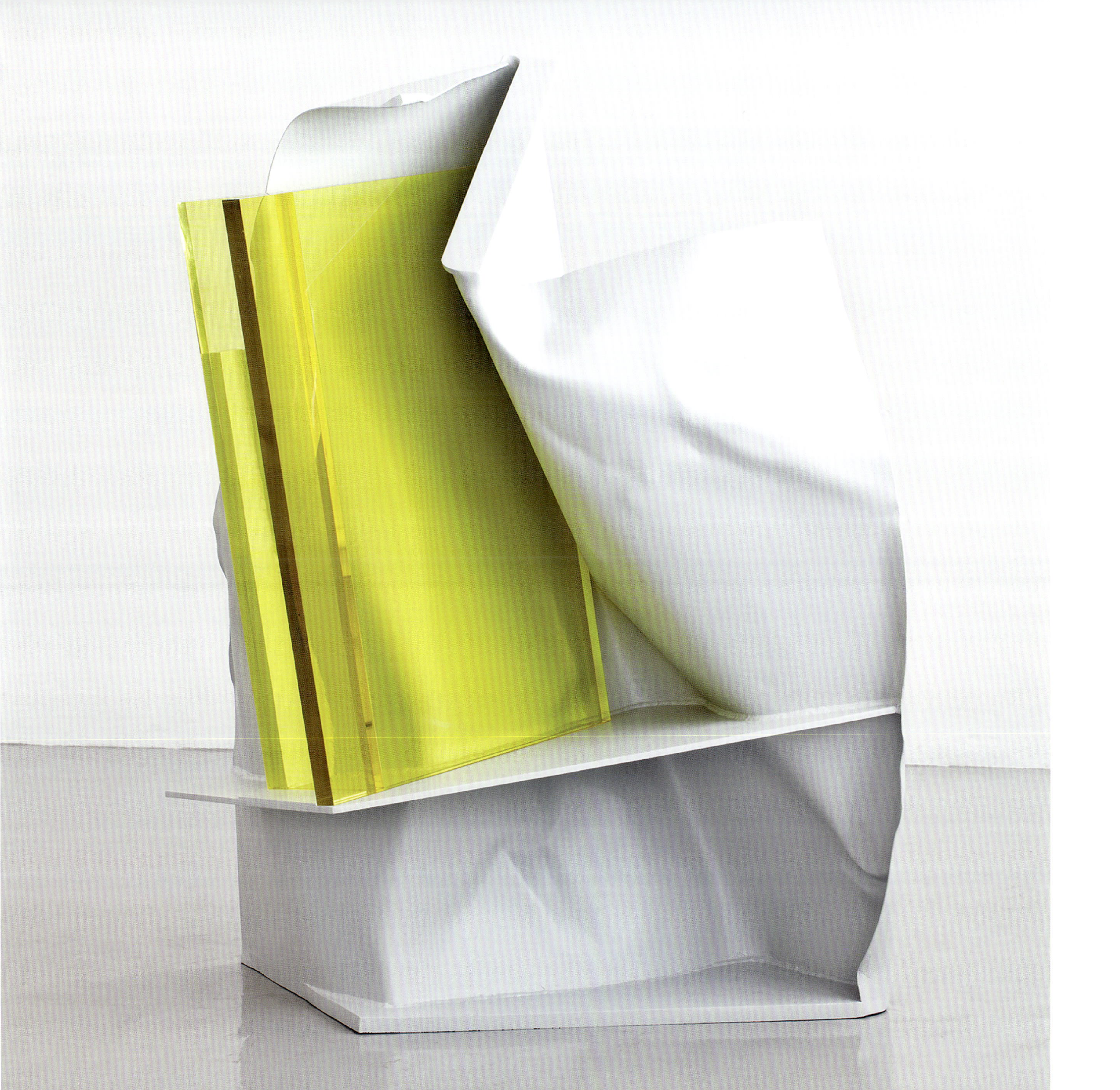

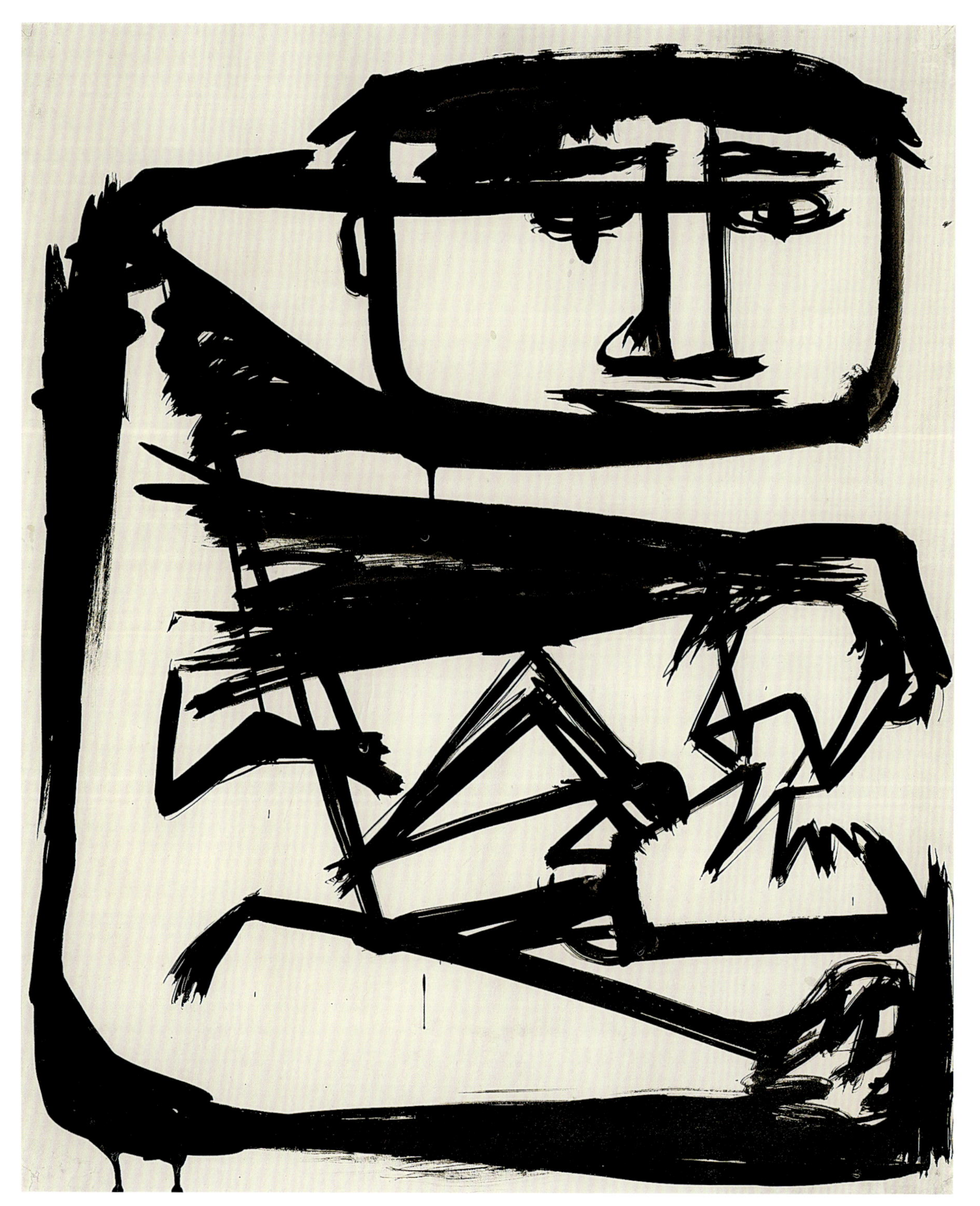

Baby With a Ball 1954

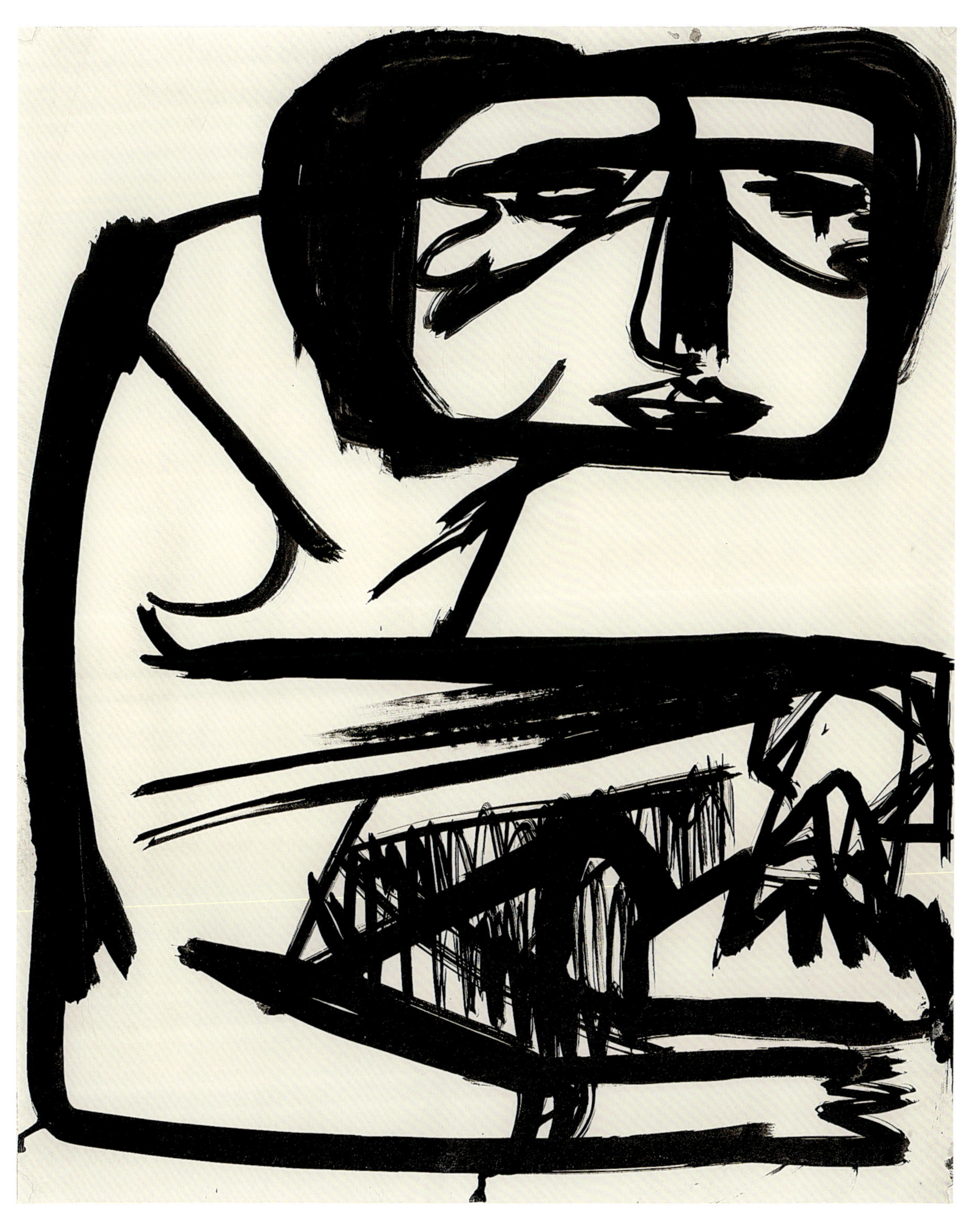

Baby With a Ball 1954

Figure 1955/1956

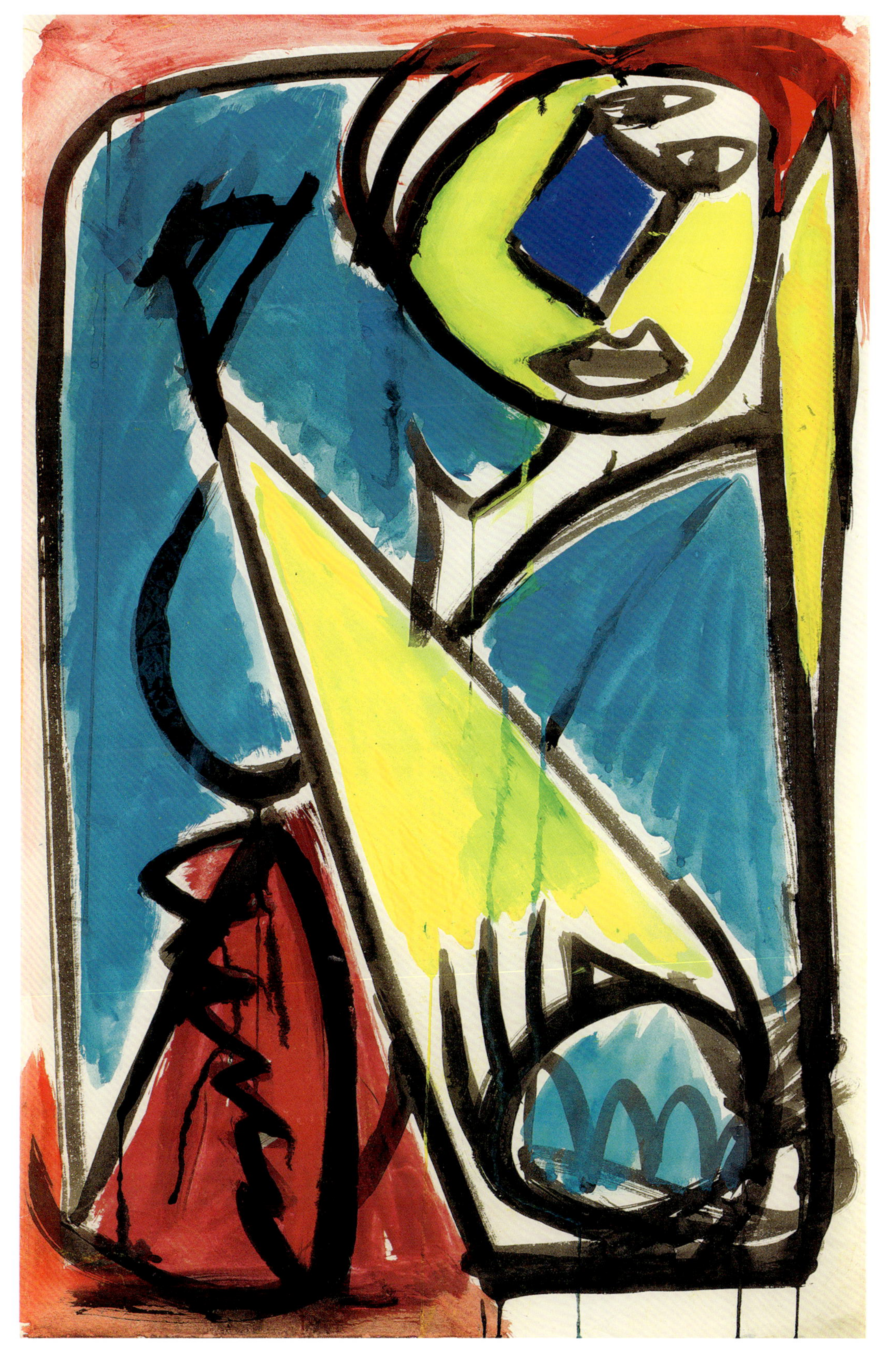

Table Piece CLIX 1973

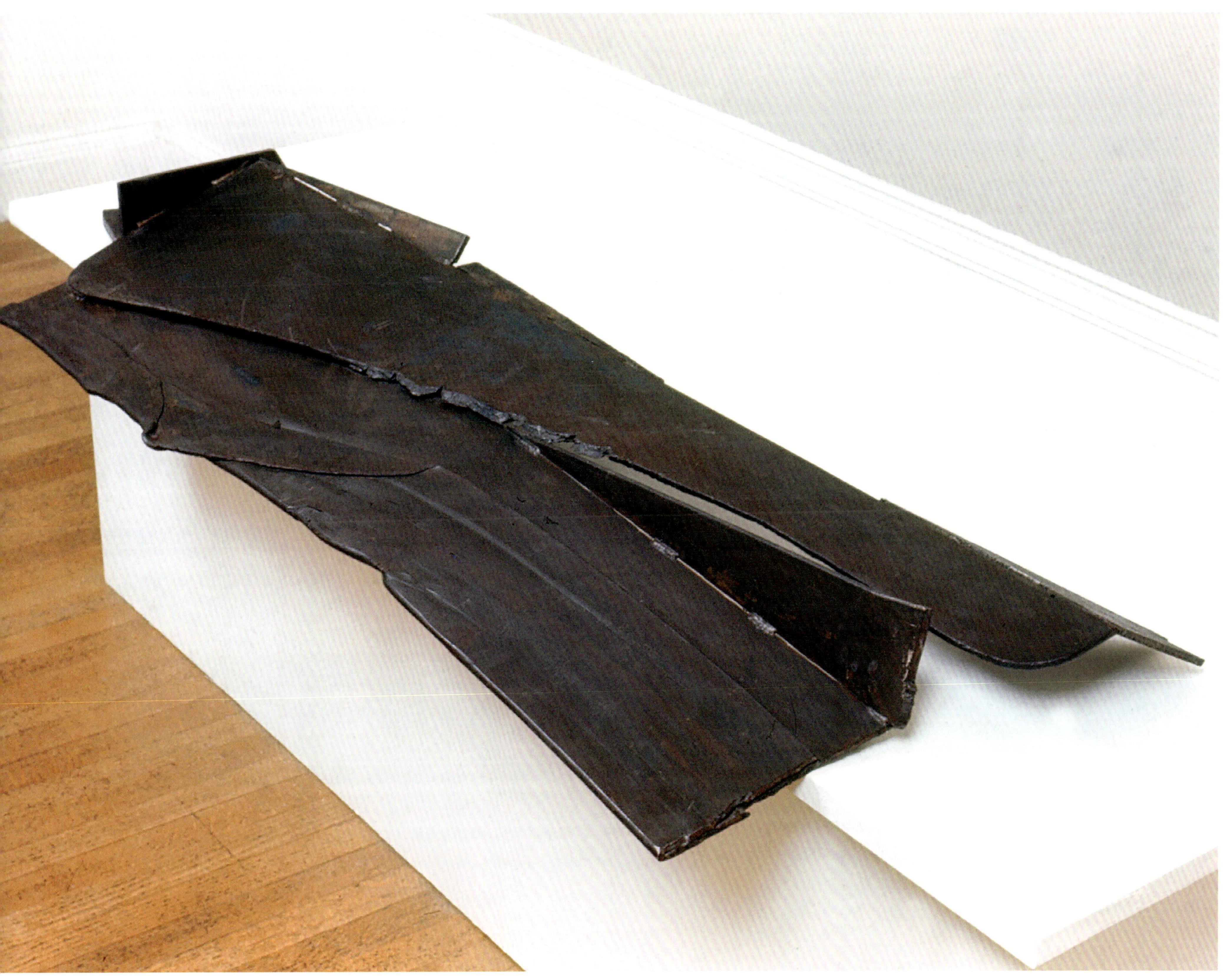

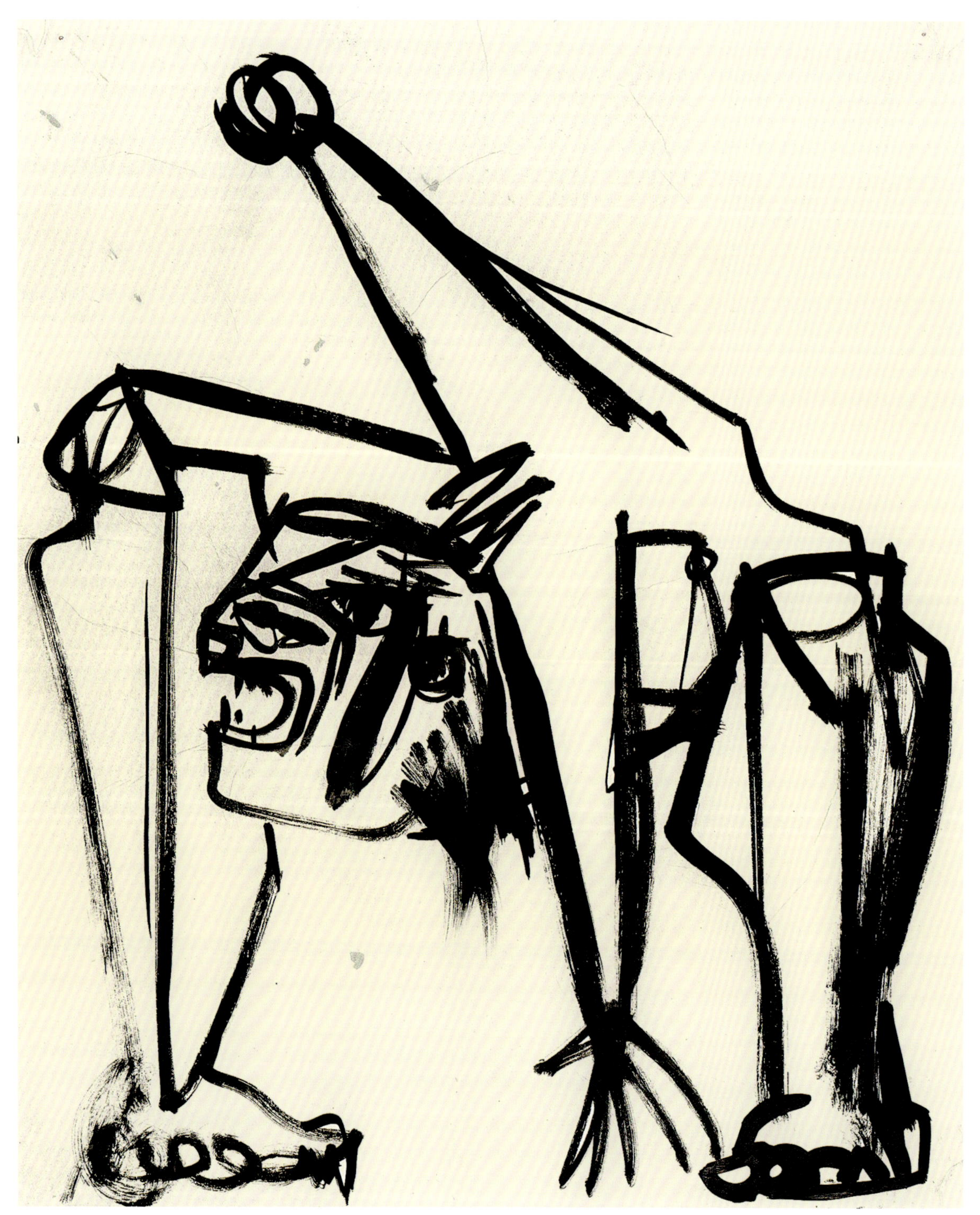

Figure 1954

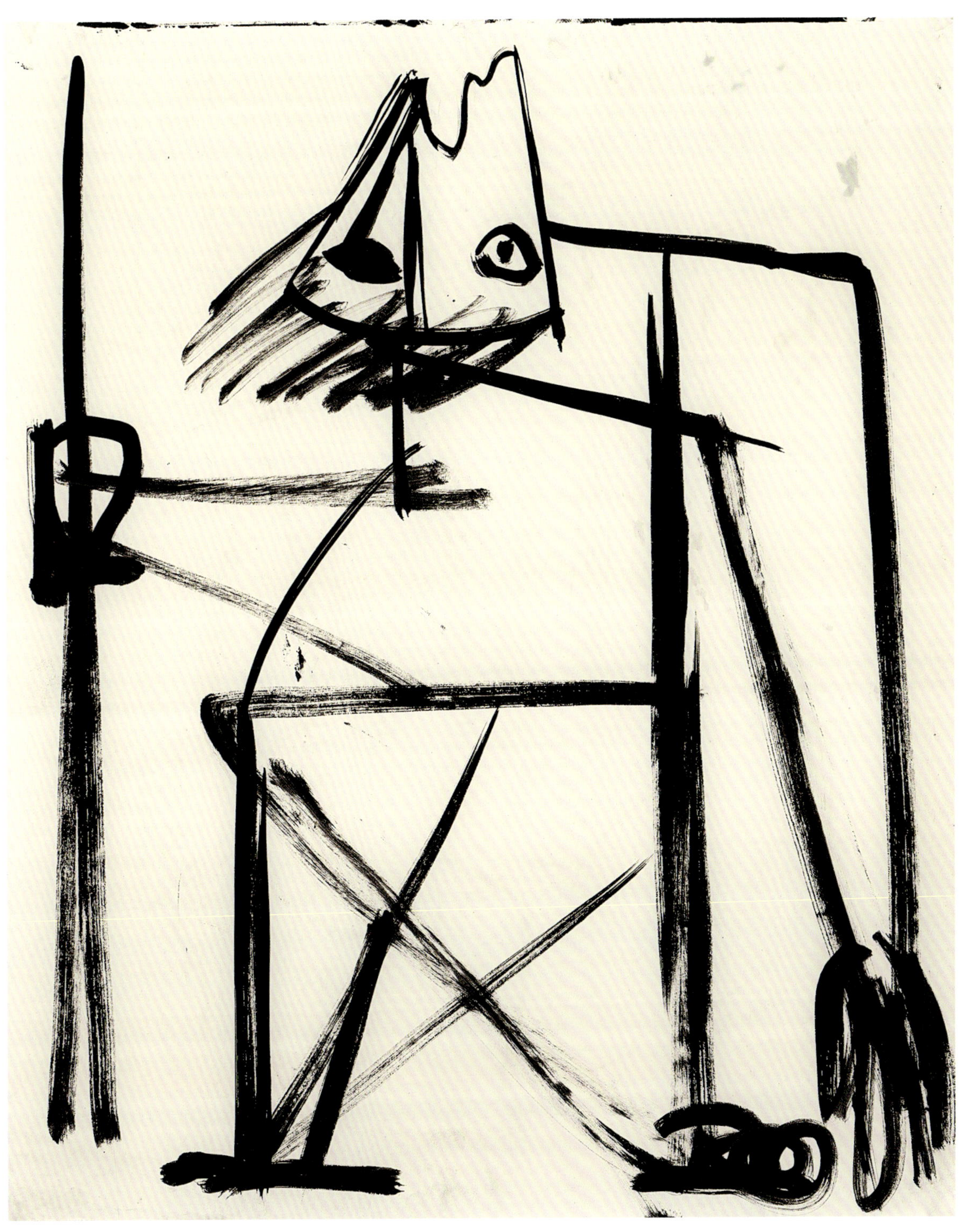

Figure 1955/1956

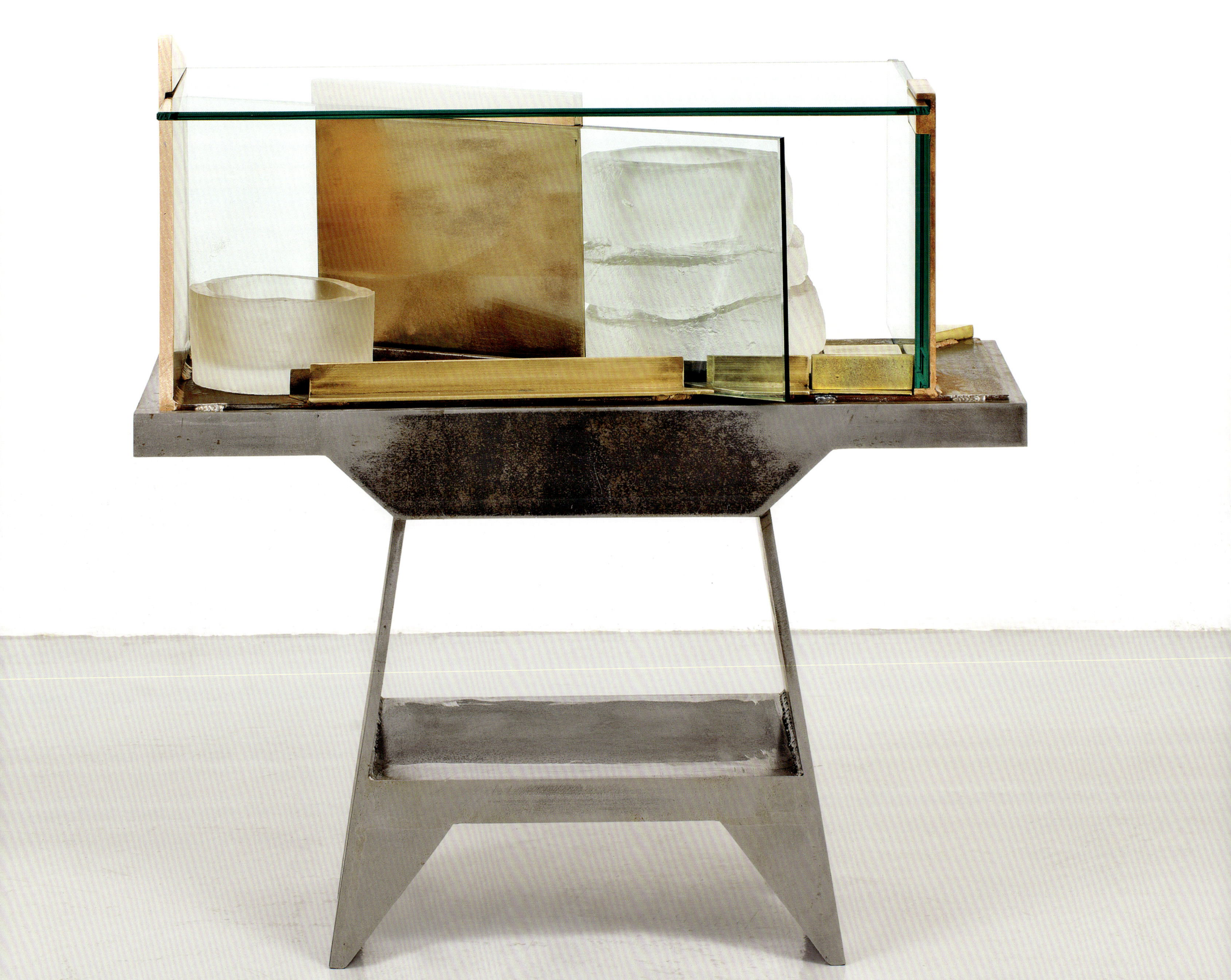

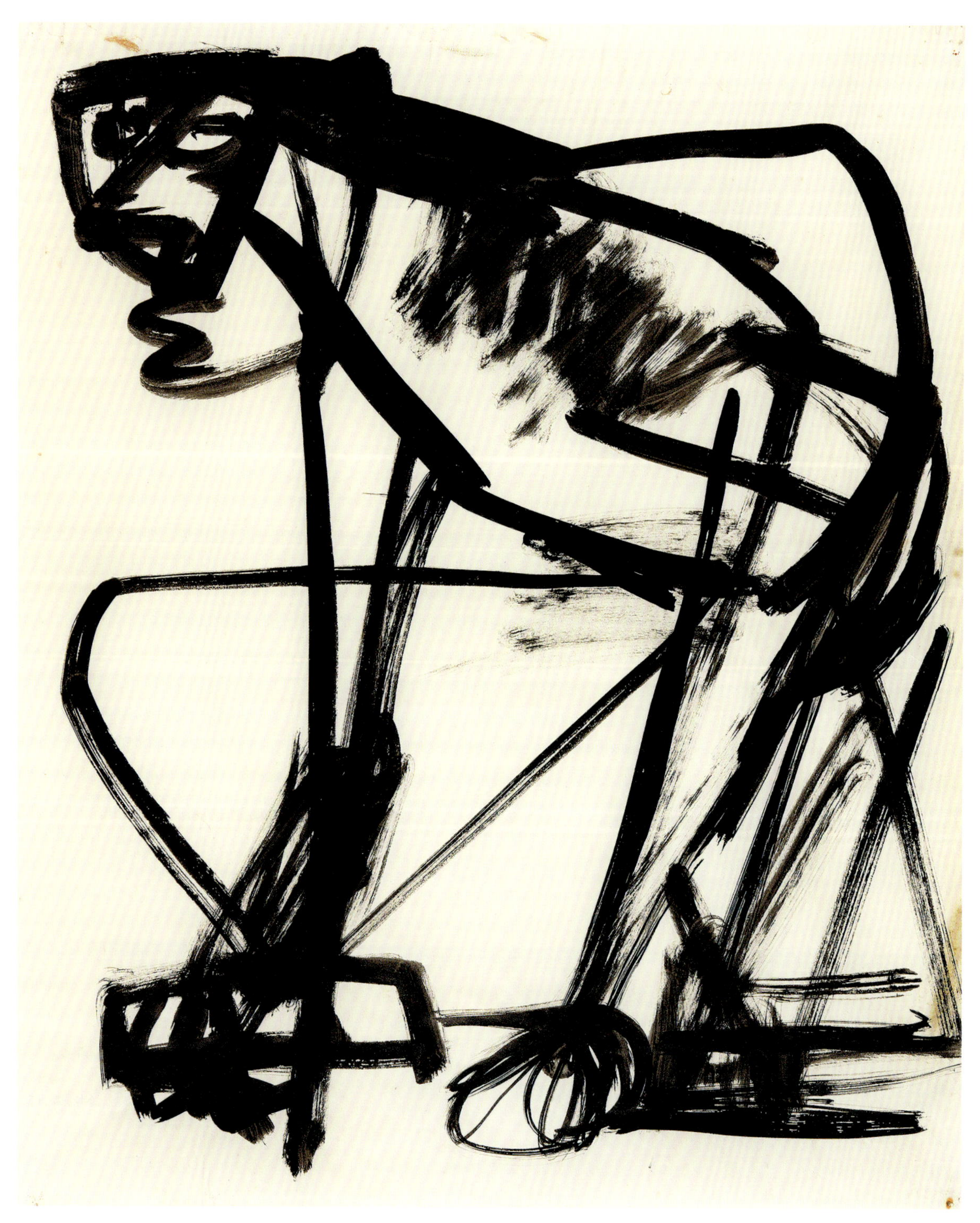

Figure 1954

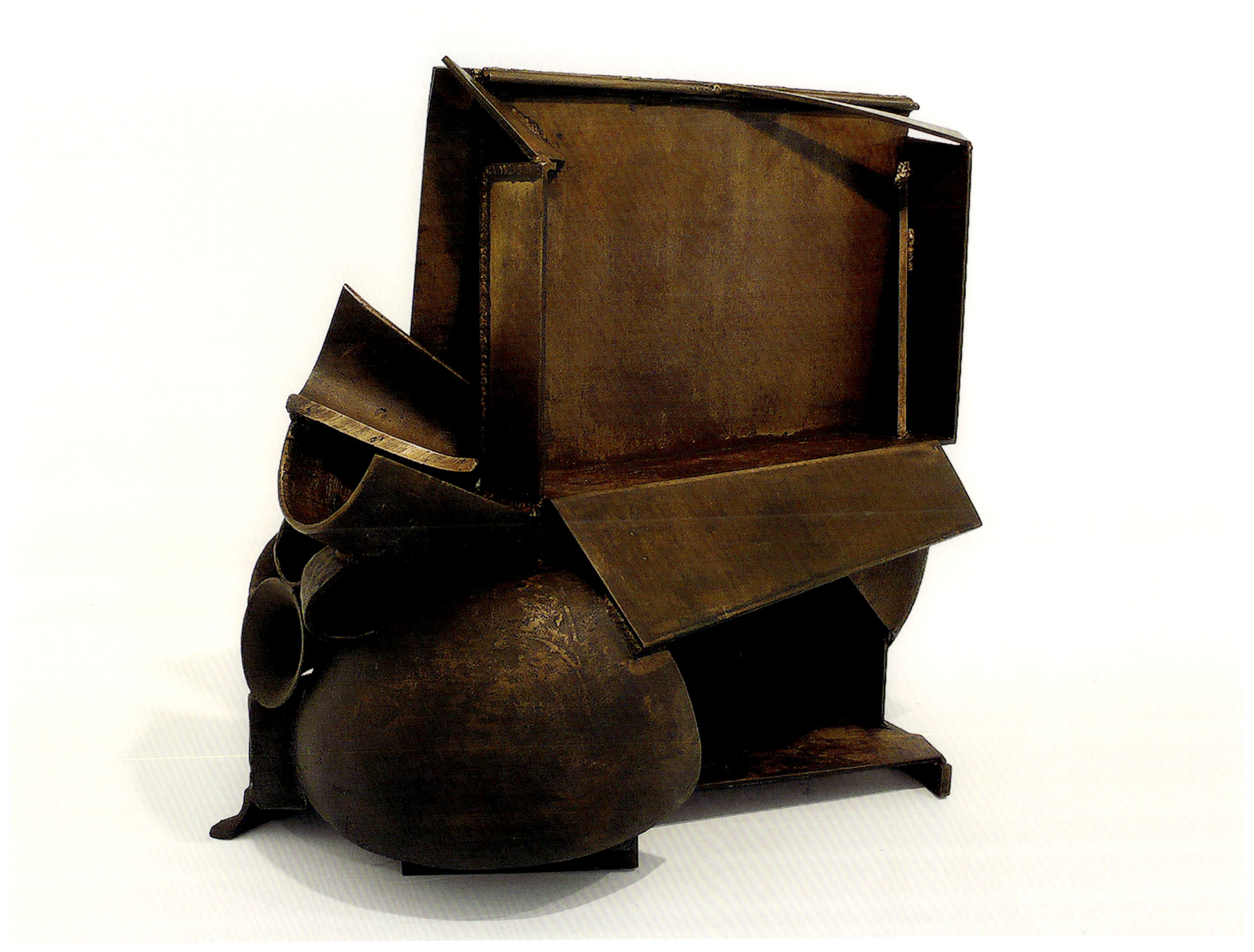

Halved 1980/1981

Figure 1955/1956

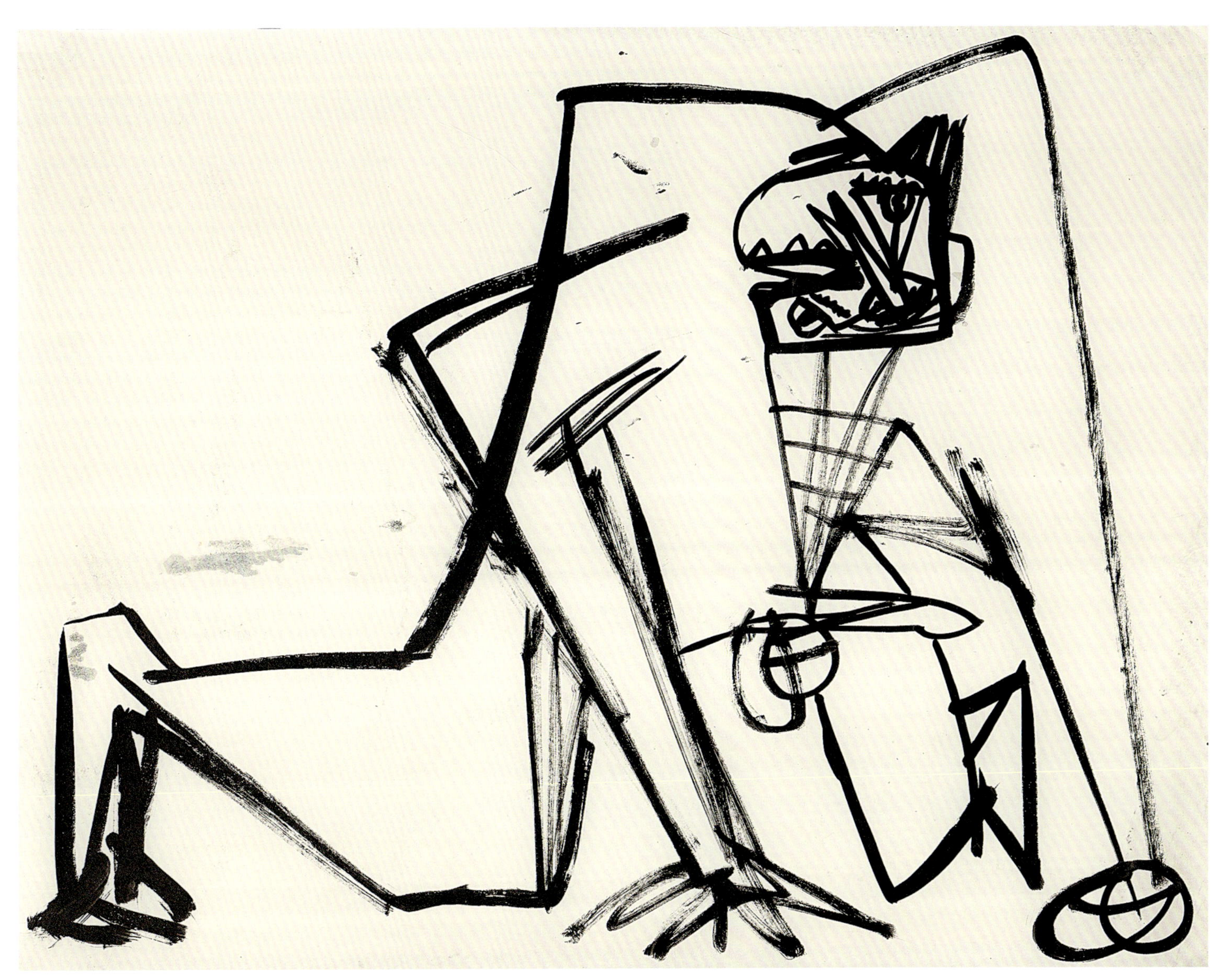

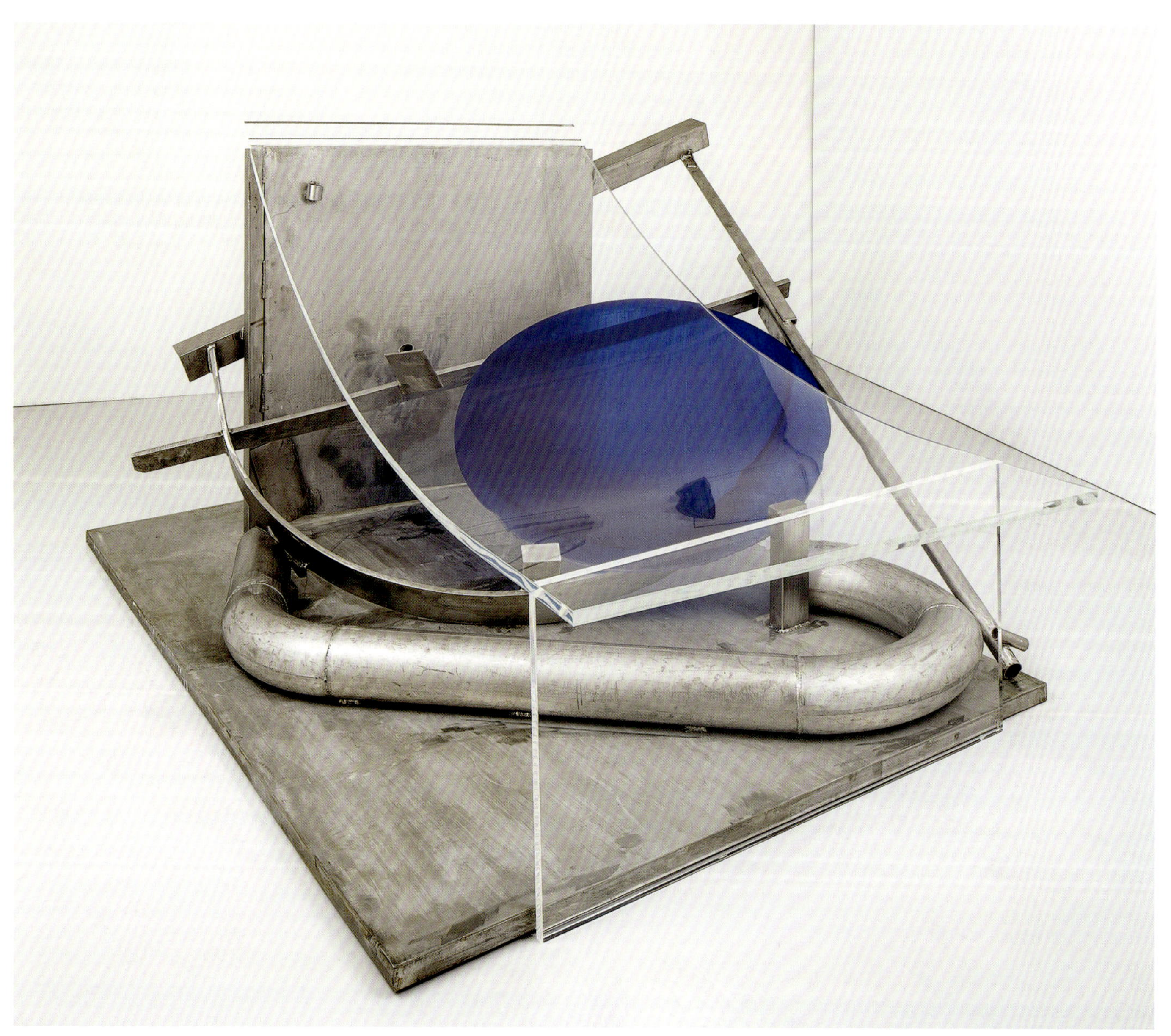

Blue Moon 2013

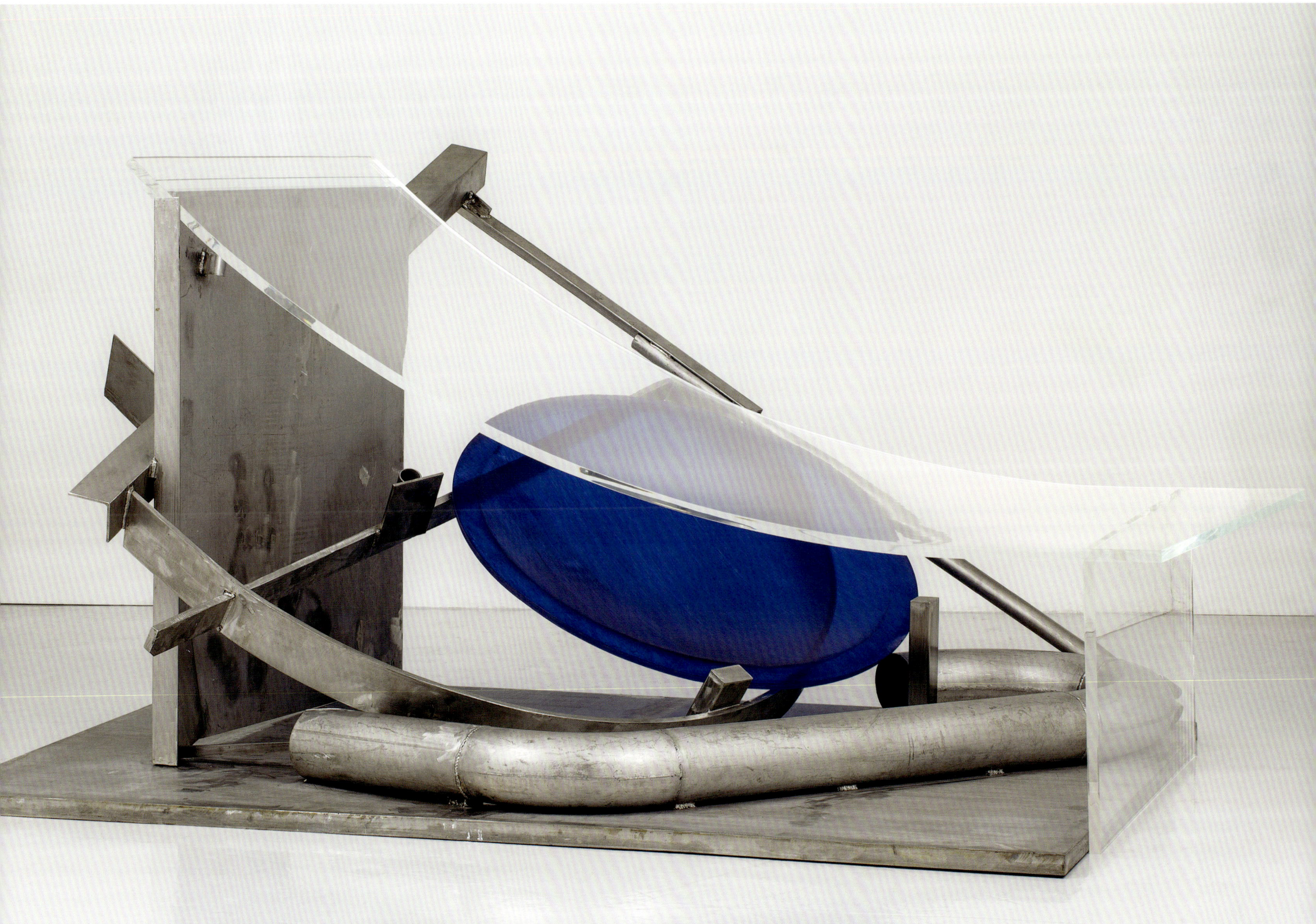

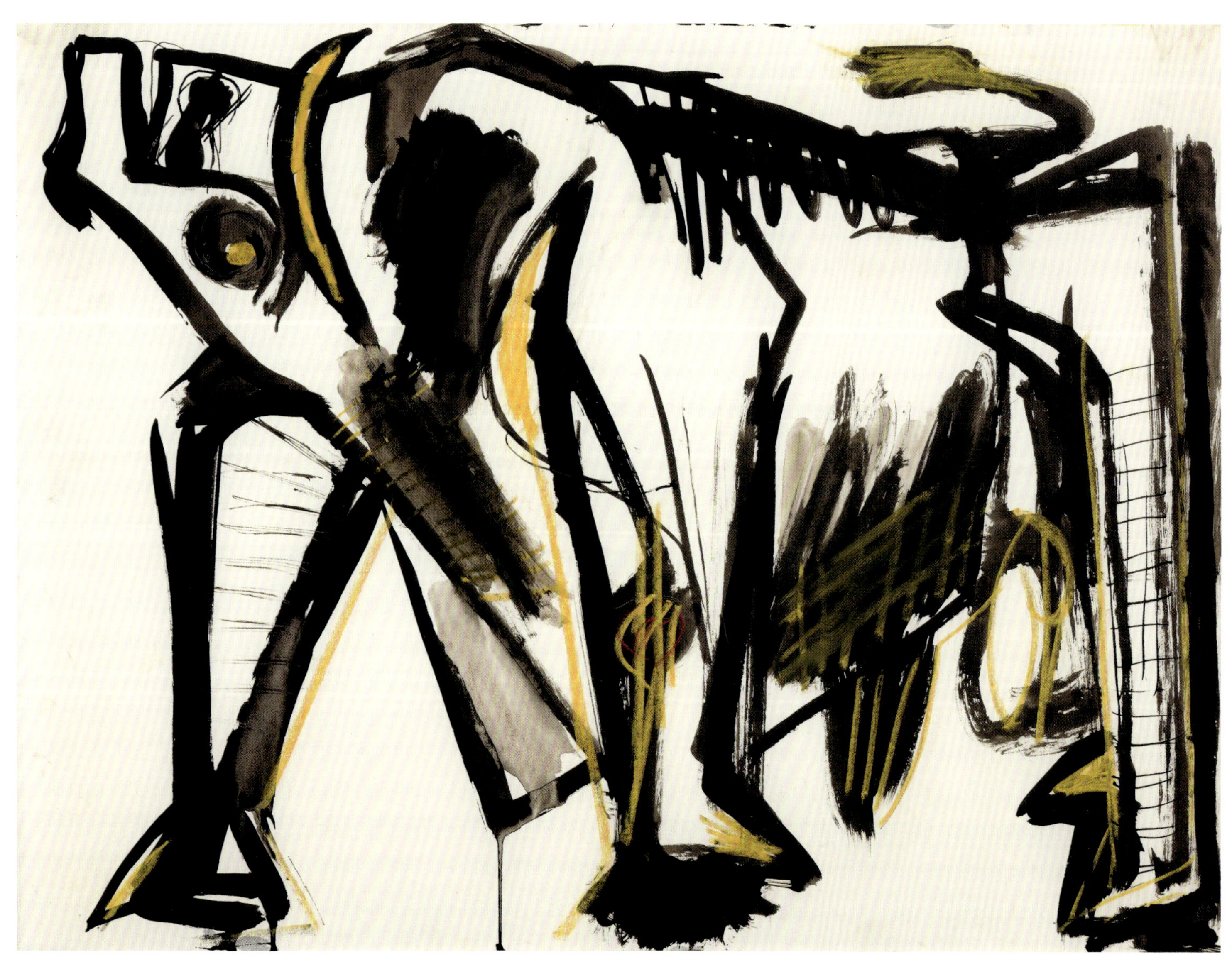

Bull 1954

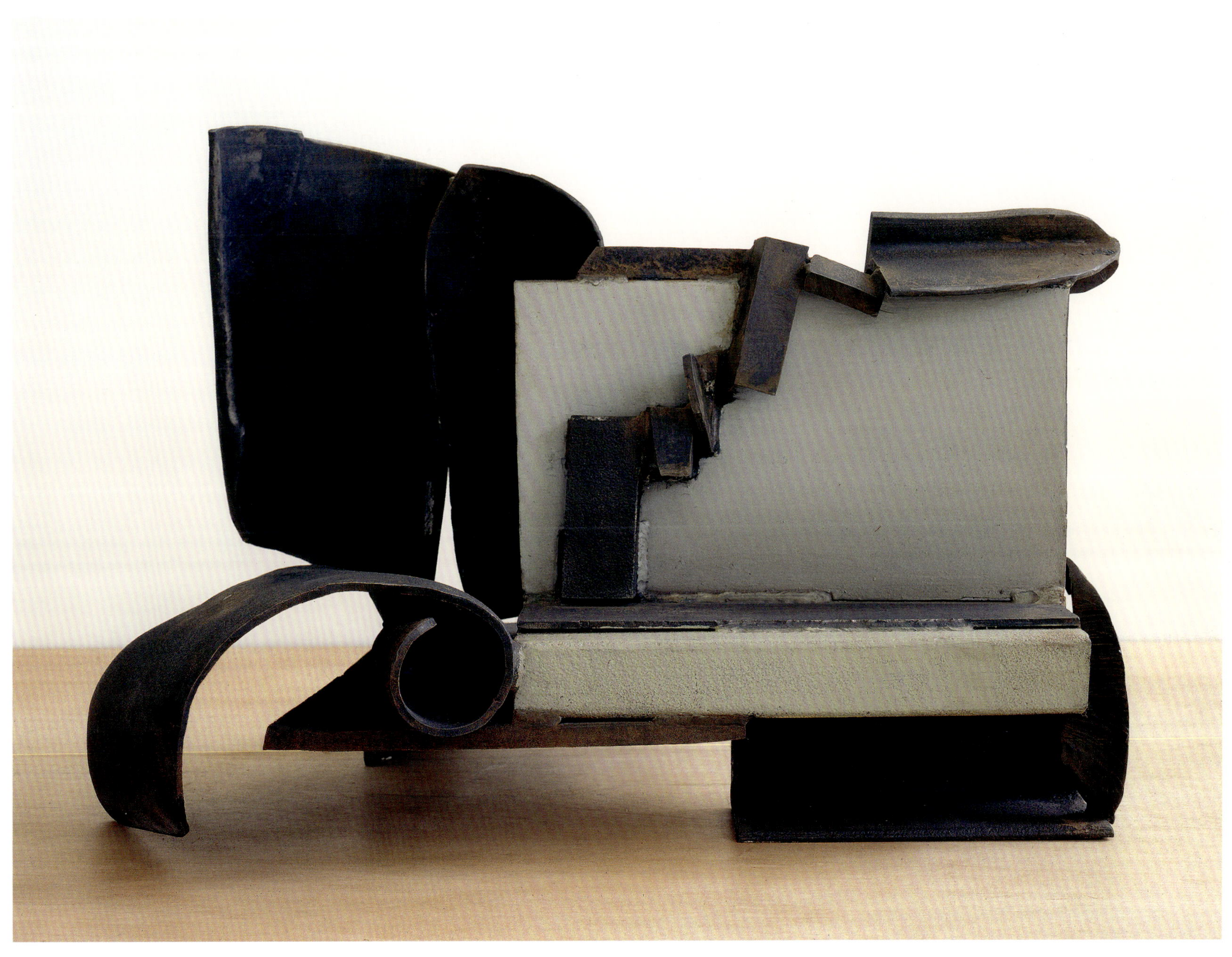

Table Piece Y-55 'No Talking' 1985/1986

Bull 1954

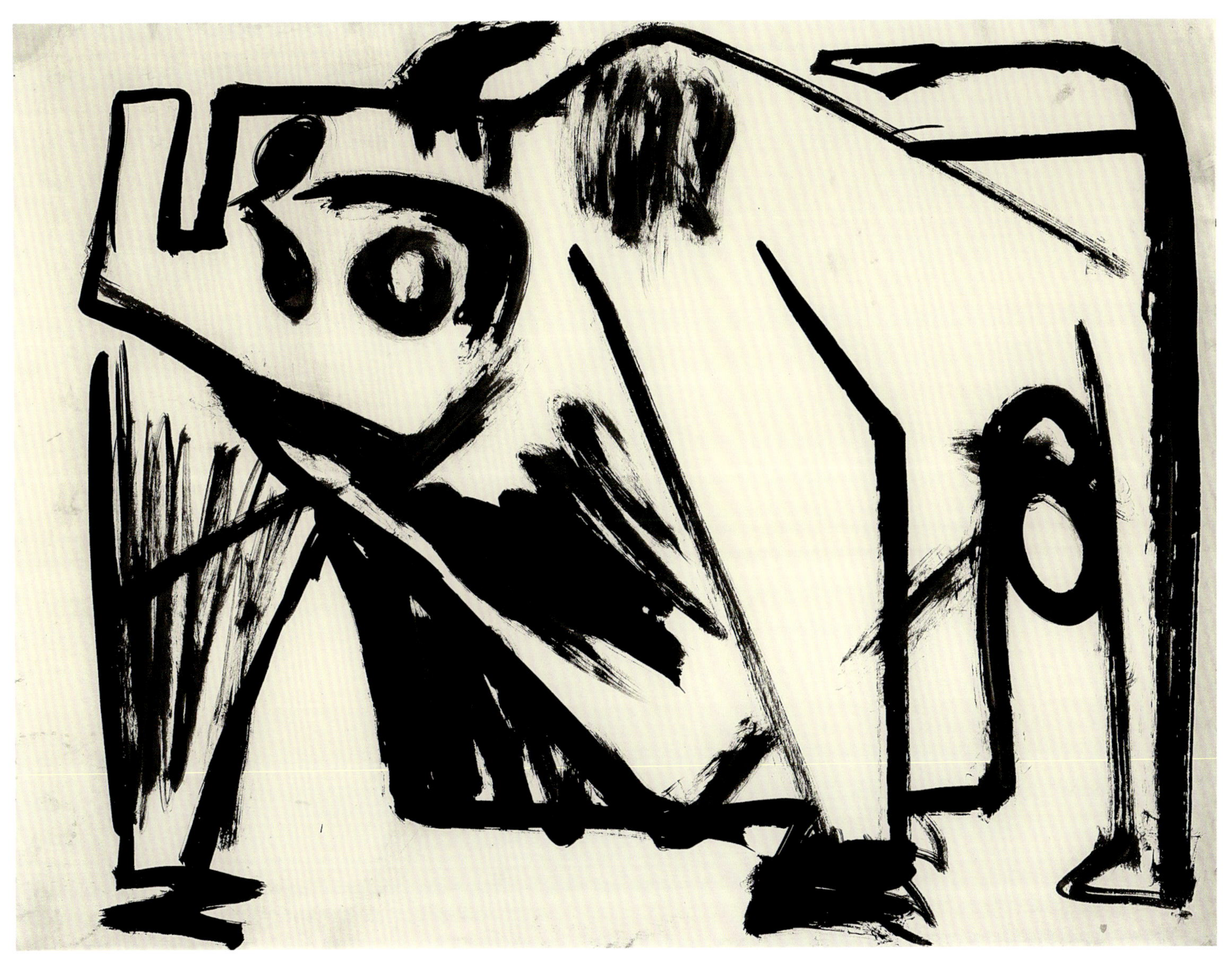

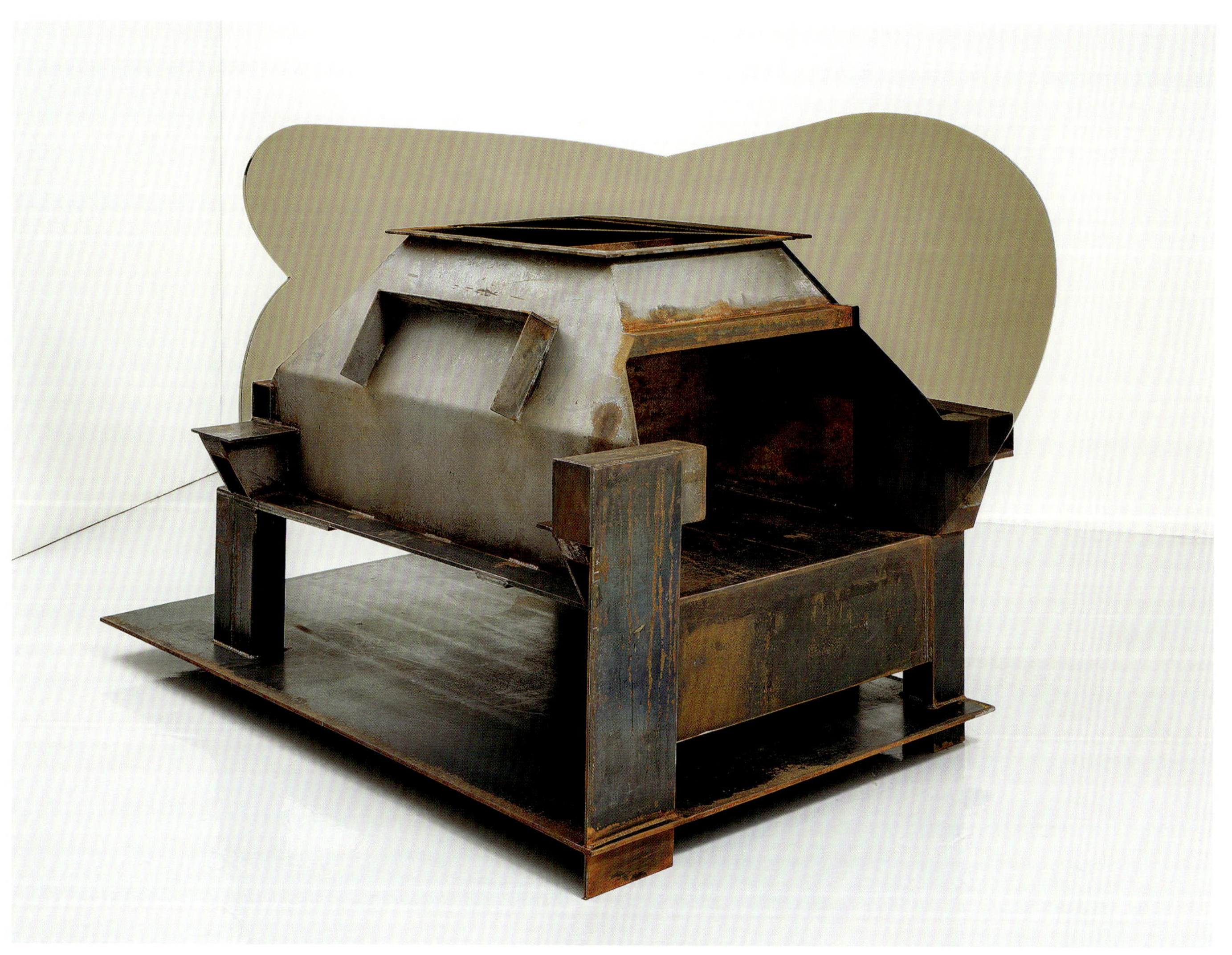

Sundown 2013

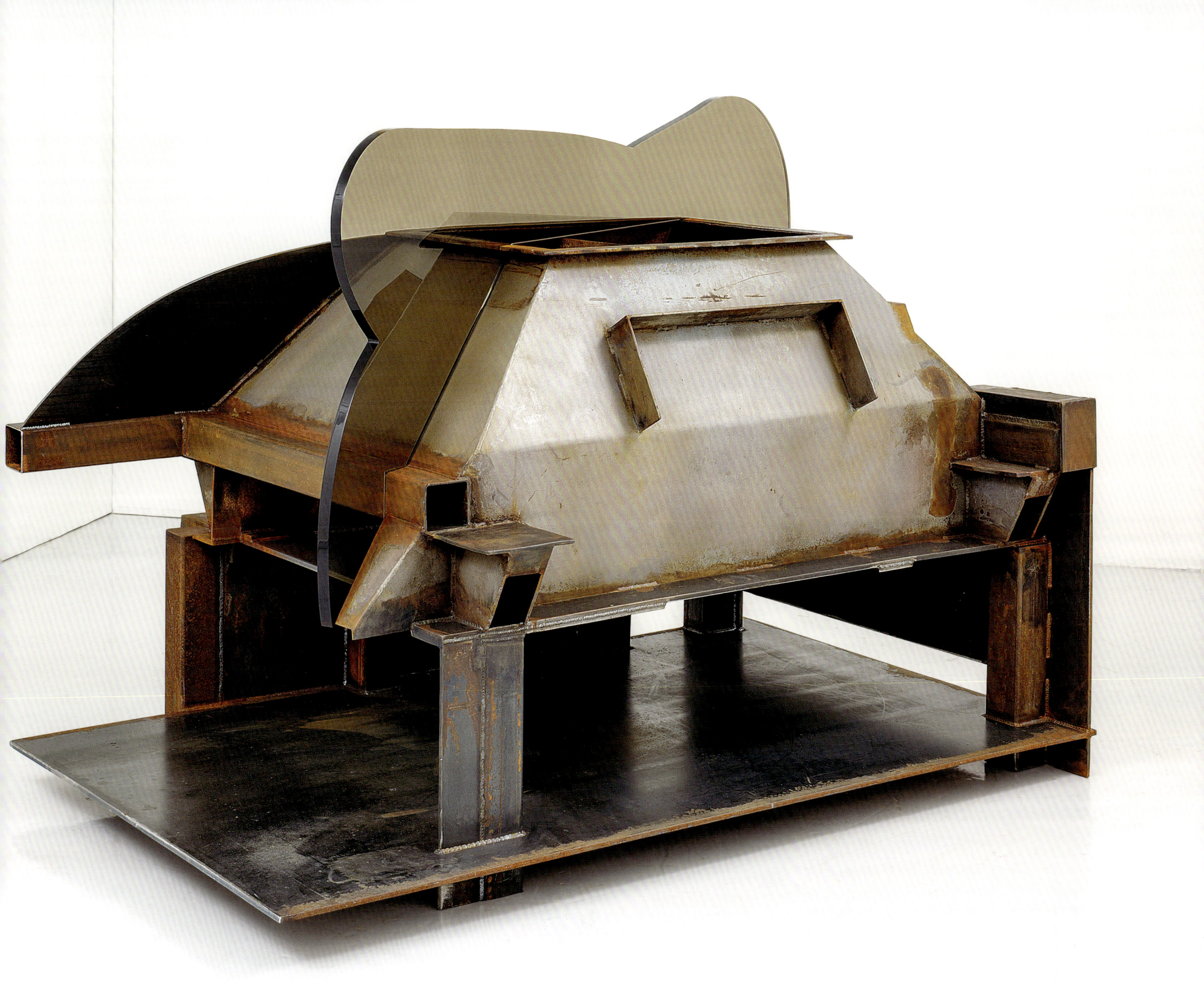

Bull 1954

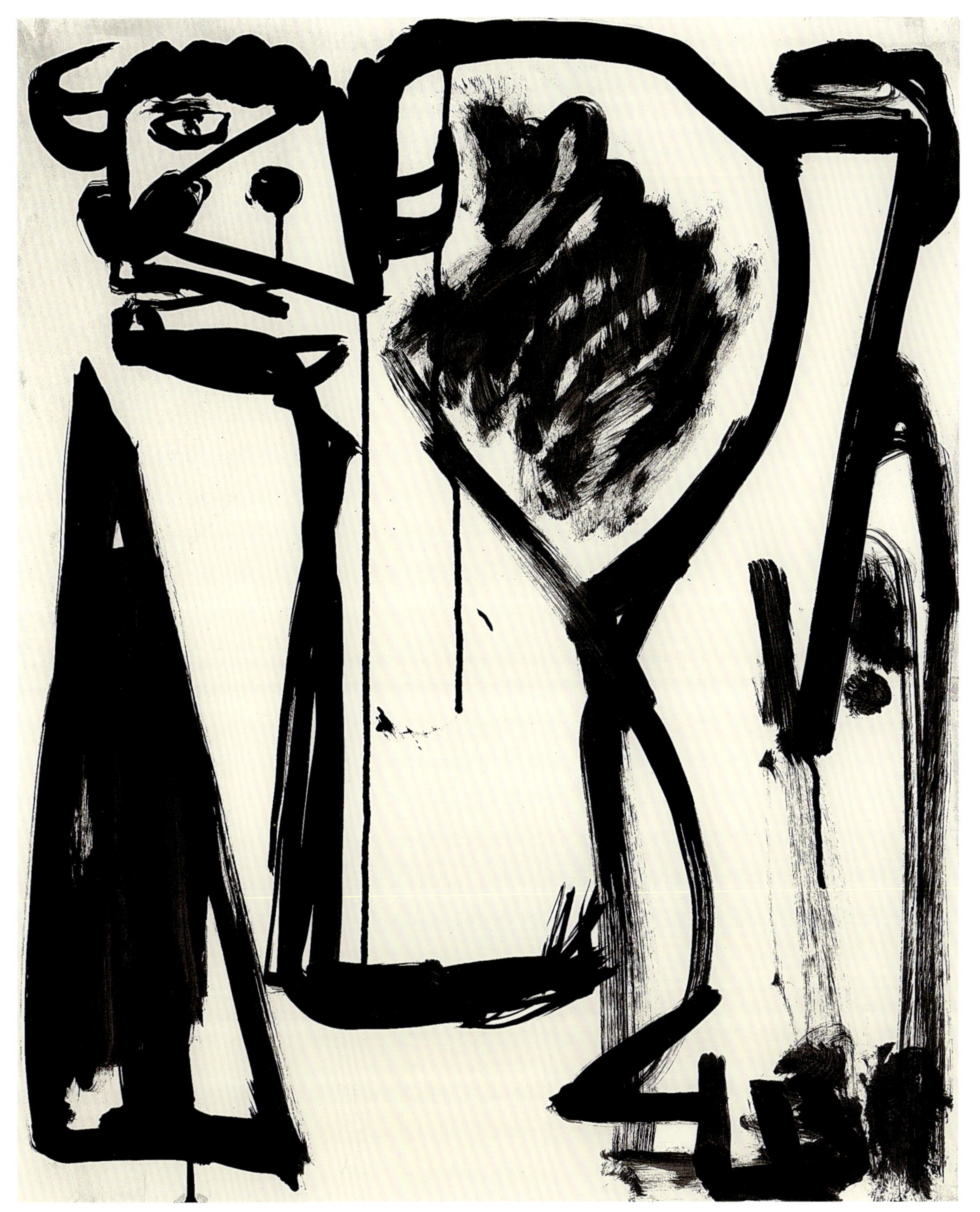

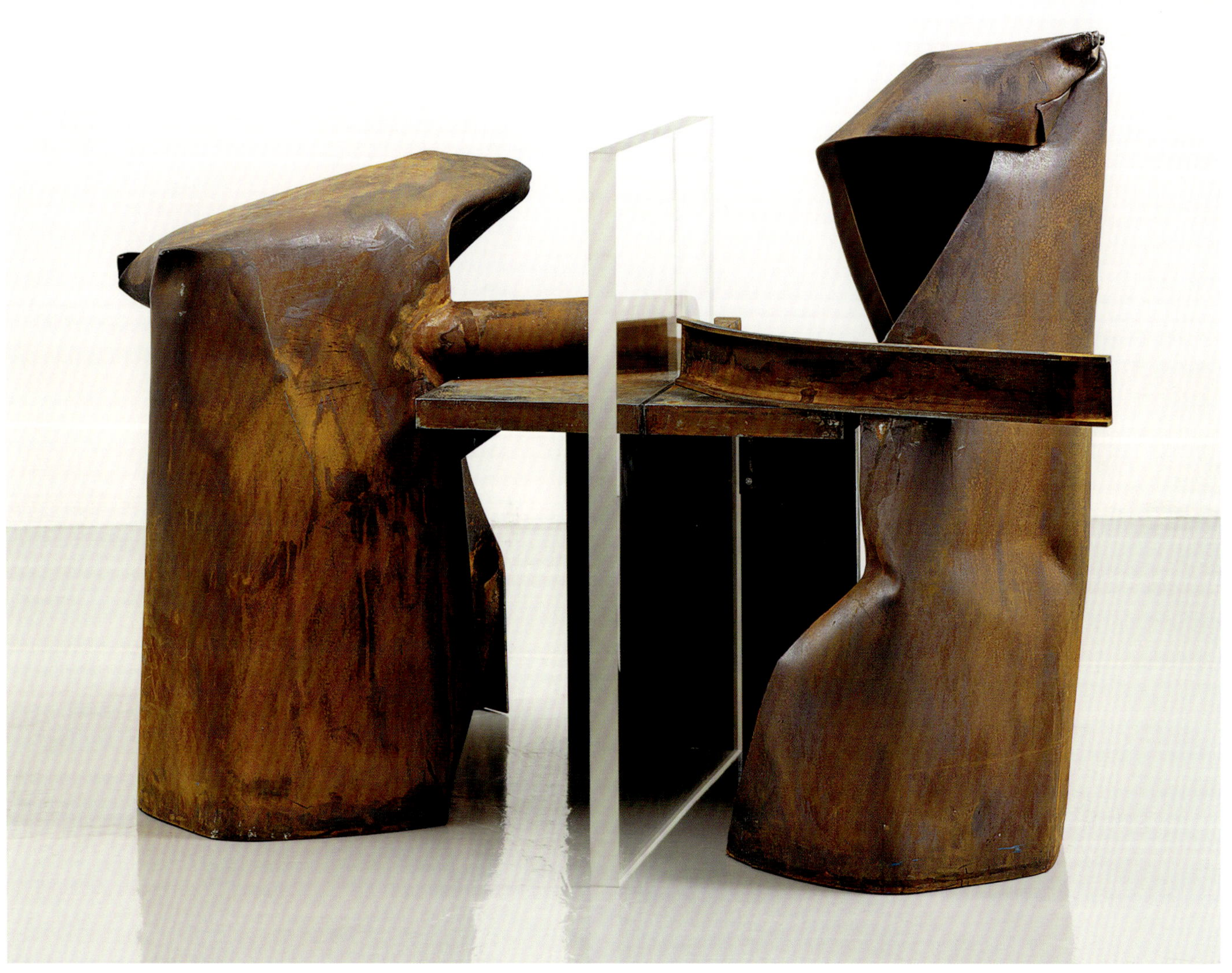

Sackbut 2011/2012

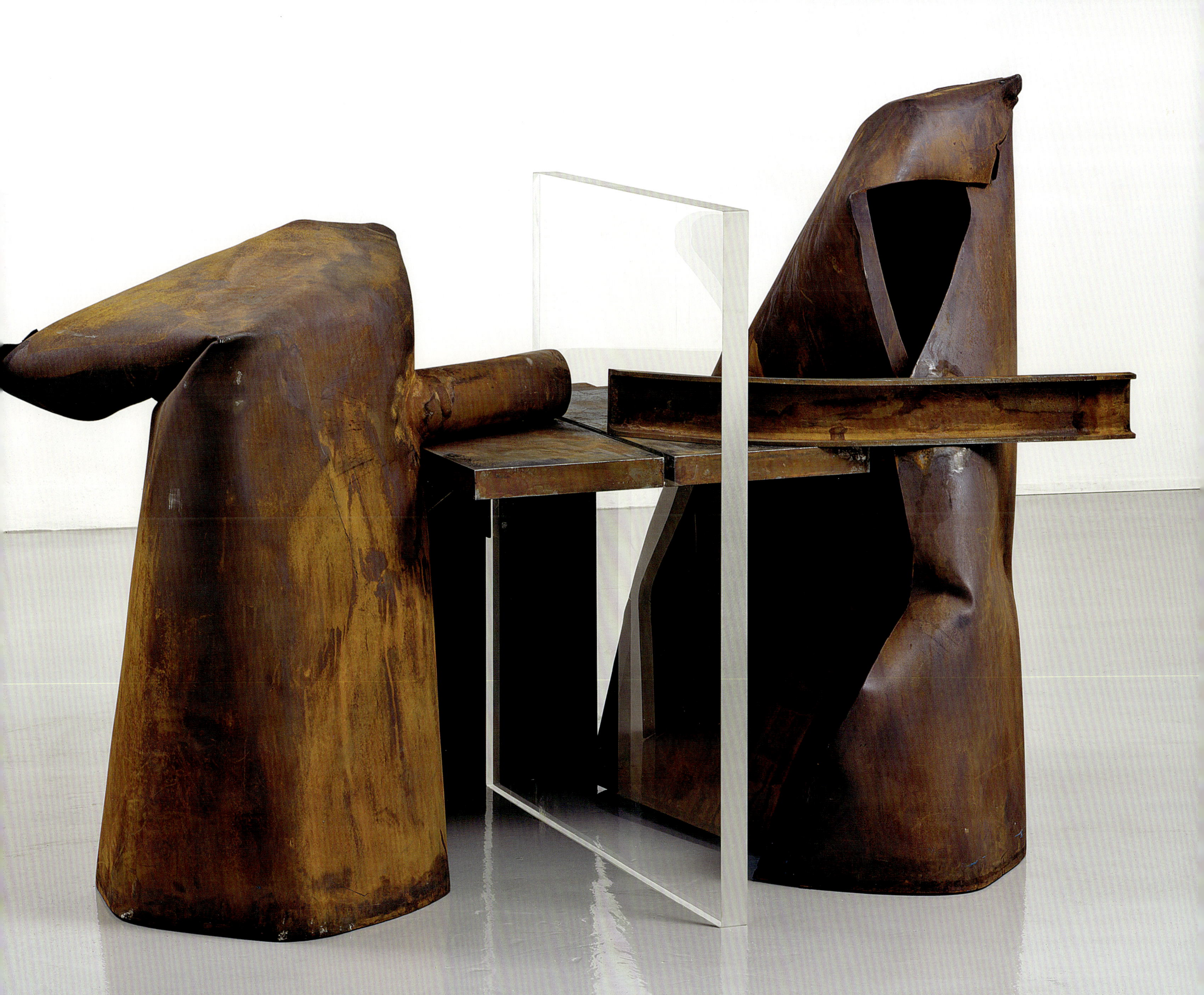

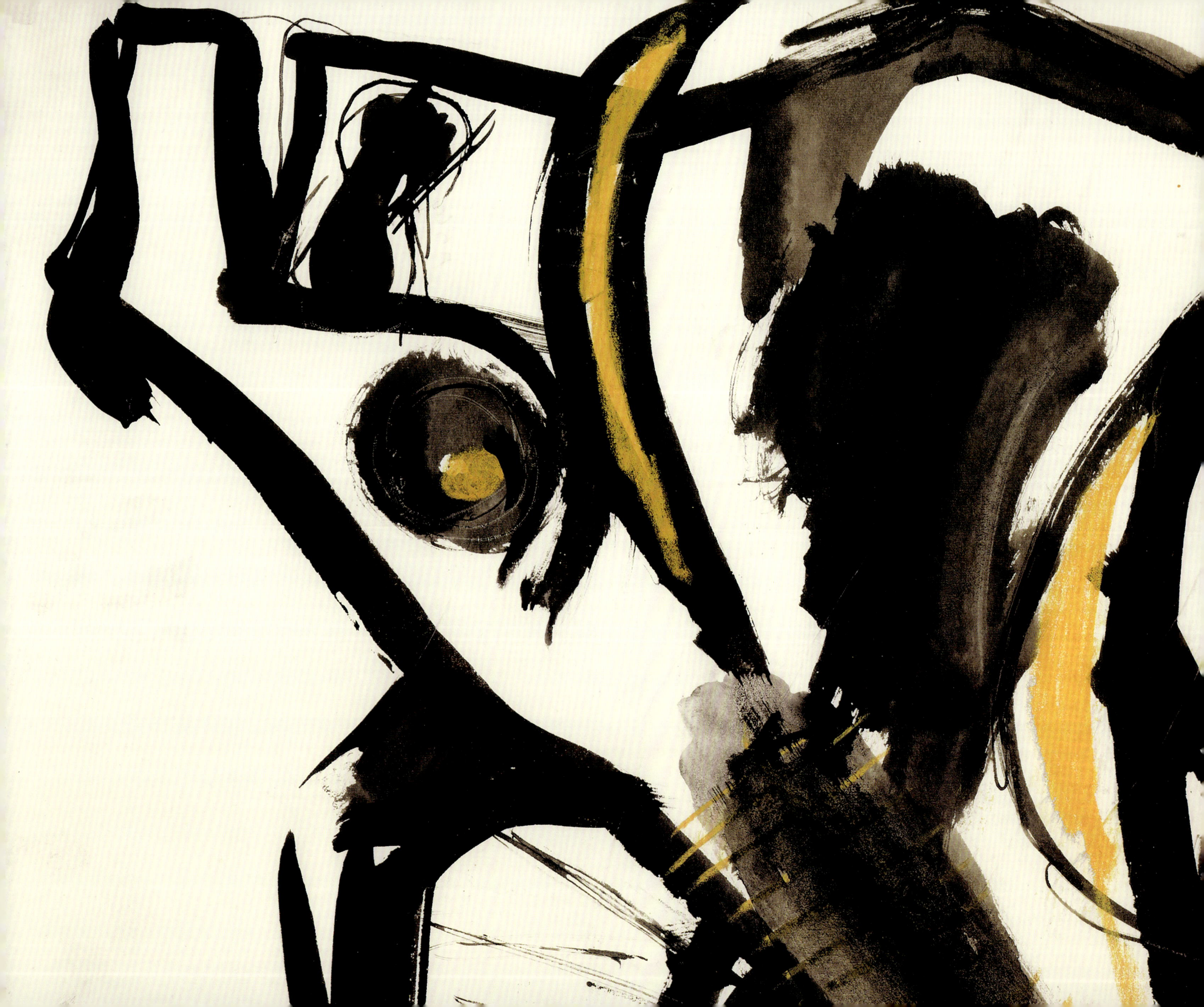

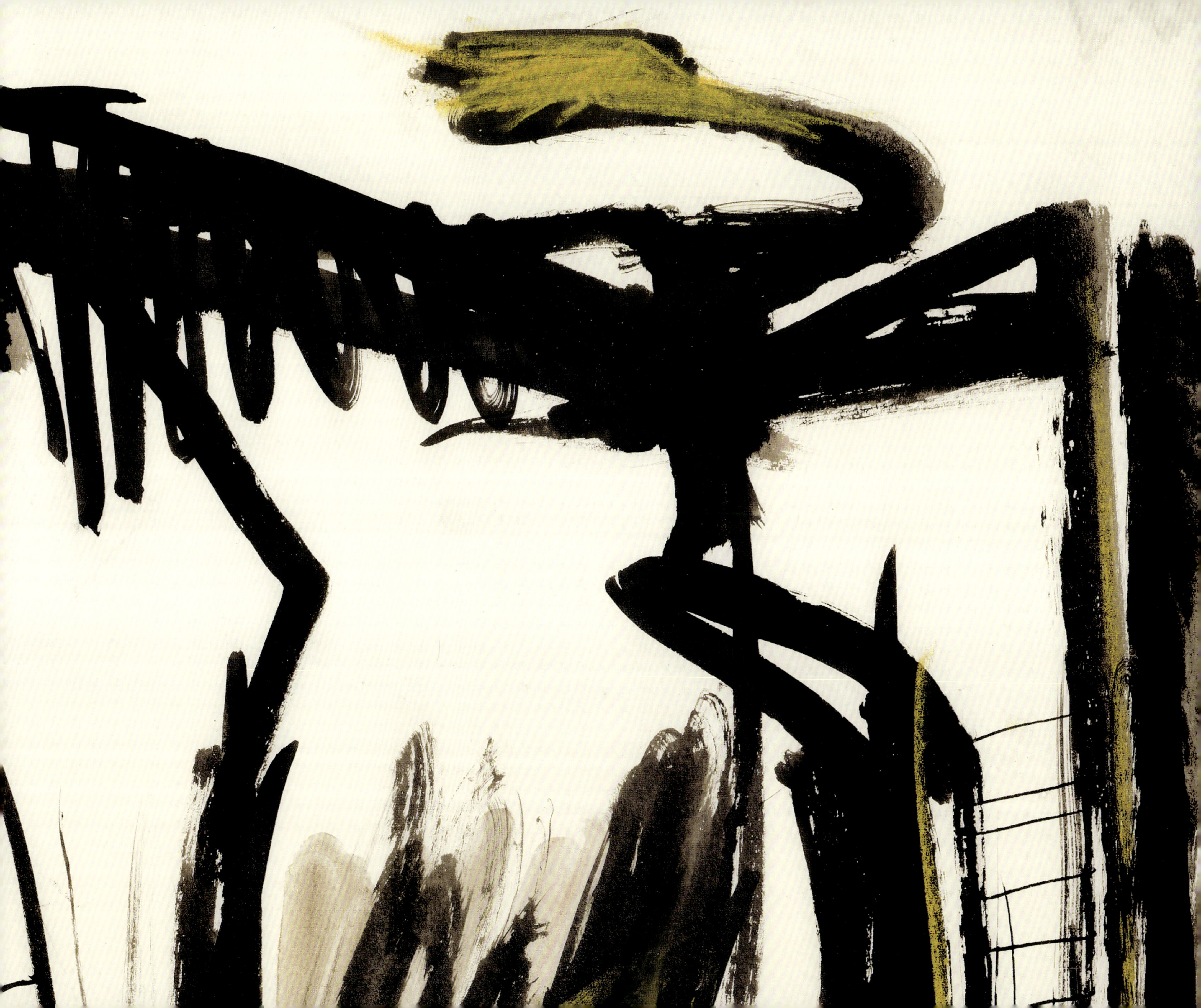

CHECKLIST

Pg 21 *Baby With a Ball*
1954, Brush and ink on newsprint
23 ⅛ x 18 inches (58.6 x 45.6 cm)

23-25 *Autumn Rhapsody*
2011/2012, Steel painted and yellow Perspex
70 x 79 ⅛ x 79 ⅛ inches (178 x 201 x 201 cm)

27 *Figure*
1955/1956, Brush, ink and paint on newsprint
33 7⁄16 x 20 ⅞ inches (85 x 53 cm)

28-29 *Terminus*
2013, Steel, jarrah wood and frosted raspberry red Perspex
63 ⅜ x 111 x 84 ⅝ inches (161 x 282 x 215 cm)

30 *Figure*
1955/1956, Brush, ink and paint on newsprint
33 x 21 inches (83.8 x 53.3 cm)

31 *Warrior*
1955/1956, Brush, ink and paint on newsprint
32 ¾ x 20 ¾ inches (83.3 x 52.9 cm)

32 *Seated Figure*
1954, Brush and ink on newsprint
21 ⅛ x 16 ½ inches (53.6 x 41.7 cm)

33 *Bull*
1954, Brush and ink on newsprint
18 ⅛ x 23 ¼ inches (46 x 59 cm)

35 *Sunlit (Table Bronze)*
1981/1982, Sheet brass, welded
20 x 22 x 19 inches (50.8 x 55.9 x 48.3 cm)

36 *Bull*
1954, Brush and ink on newsprint
18 ⅛ x 23 inches (46 x 58.4 cm)

37 *Bull*
1954, Brush and ink on newsprint
18 ½ x 23 inches (46.5 x 58.5 cm)

38-39 *Honey Suckle*
2011/2012, Beech wood
40 x 36 ½ x 18 ½ inches (101.6 x 92.7 x 47 cm)

40 *Baby With a Ball*
1954, Brush and ink on newsprint
23 ⅛ x 18 inches (58.6 x 45.6 cm)

41 *Baby With a Ball*
1954, Brush and ink on newsprint
23 ⅛ x 18 inches (58.7 x 45.6 cm)

42-43 *Alpine*
2012, Steel and yellow Perspex
59 ½ x 49 ¼ x 26 inches (151.1 x 125.1 x 66 cm)

44 *Baby With a Ball*
1954, Brush and ink on newsprint
23 x 18 inches (58.3 x 45.8 cm)

45 *Baby With a Ball*
1954, Brush and ink on newsprint
23 x 18 inches (58.4 x 45.6 cm)

47 *Figure*
1955/1956, Brush, ink and paint on newsprint
32 ¾ x 20 ¾ inches (83.4 x 52.9 cm)

49 *Table Piece CLIX*
1973, Steel, varnished
7 ½ x 73 x 27 inches (19.1 x 185.4 x 68.6 cm)

50 *Figure*
1954, Brush and ink on newsprint
23 x 17 ¾ inches (58.3 x 45.2 cm)

51 *Figure*
1955/1956, Brush and ink on newsprint
32 ¾ x 21 inches (83.4 x 53.1 cm)

53 *Display*
2011/2012, Glass, bronze and steel
33 x 30 ⅜ x 14 ½ inches (83.8 x 73.7 x 38.1 cm)

54 *Figure*
1954, Brush and ink on newsprint
21 x 16 ½ inches (53.4 x 41.6 cm)

55 *Halved*
1980/1981, Bronze and brass, cast and welded
29 x 33 x 16 inches (73.7 x 83.8 x 40.6 cm)

57 *Figure*
1955/1956, Brush and ink on newsprint
18 x 23 inches (45.8 x 58.2 cm)

58-59 *Blue Moon*
2013, Stainless steel, clear Perspex and
clear Perspex, painted
54 x 90 x 103 inches (137 x 228.6 x 261.6 cm)

60 *Bull*
1954, Brush, ink and crayon on newsprint
18 ⅛ x 23 ⅛ inches (46 x 58.6 cm)

61 *Table Piece Y-55 'No Talking'*
1985/1986, Steel, painted and varnished
19 ½ x 28 x 18 inches (49.5 x 71.1 x 45.7 cm)

63 *Bull*
1954, Brush and ink on newsprint
18 ⅛ x 23 inches (46.1 x 58.6 cm)

64-65 *Sundown*
2013, Steel and neutral Perspex
60 ⅝ x 85 x 56 ⅜ inches (154 x 216 x 143 cm)

67 *Bull*
1954, Brush and ink on newsprint
23 x 18 ⅛ inches (58.5 x 46.1 cm)

68-69 *Sackbut*
2011/2012, Steel and clear Perspex and steel,
rusted and waxed
48 x 70 x 46 inches (122 x 178 x 117 cm)

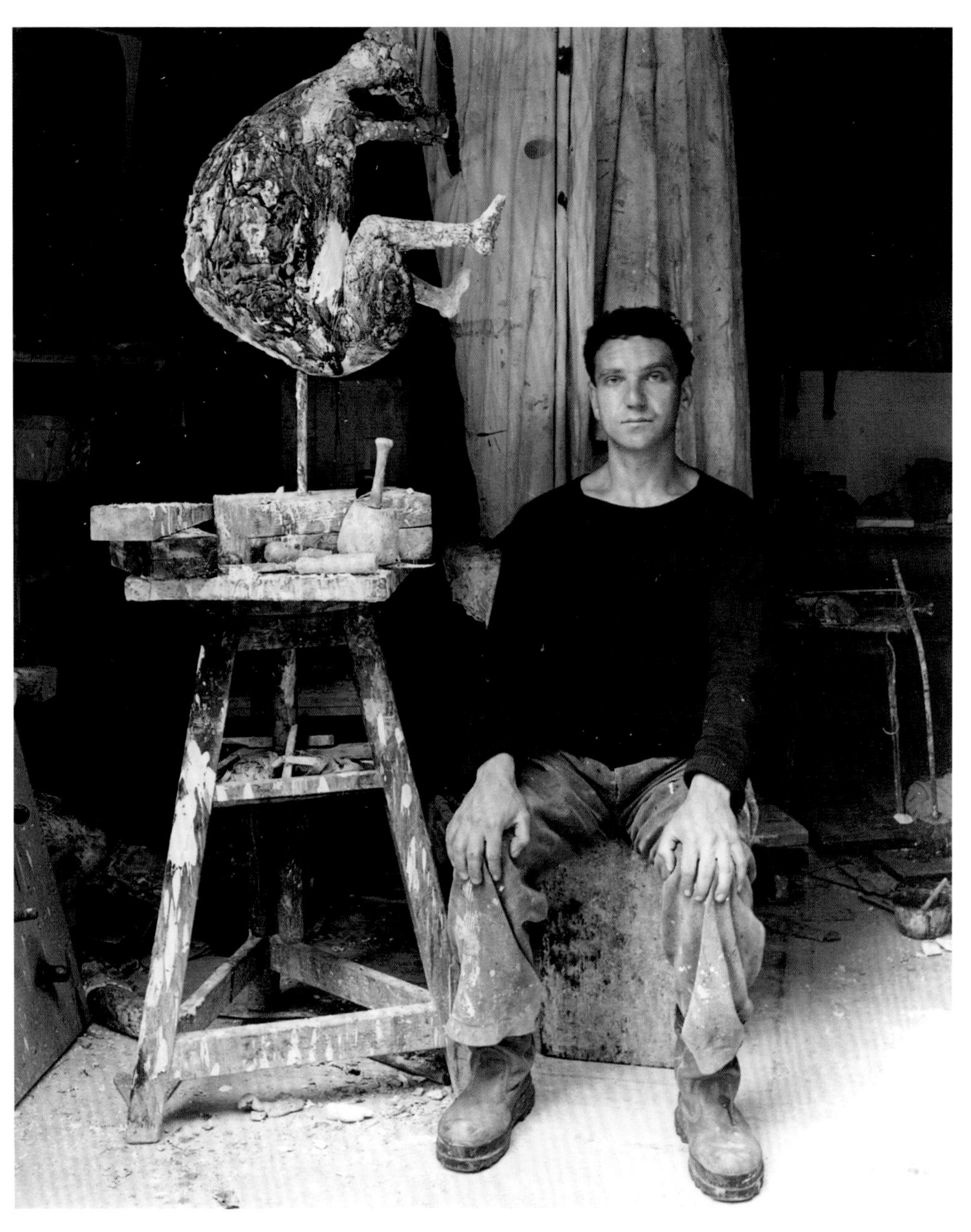

Portrait of Anthony Caro, 1957

ILLUSTRATIONS

Cover
Figure (detail)
1955/1956, Brush, ink and paint on newsprint
33 7/16 x 20 7/8 inches (85 x 53 cm)

Pages 2-3
Bull (detail)
1954, Brush and ink on newsprint
18 1/8 x 23 inches (46 x 58.4 cm)

Page 4
Man Holding His Foot, 1954 and *Warrior*, 1955/1956
in Caro's studio at his home in Hampstead, ca. 1955

Page 8
Autumn Rhapsody (detail)
2011/2012, Steel, painted and yellow Perspex
70 x 79 1/8 x 79 1/8 inches (178 x 201 x 201 cm)

Page 11
Man Holding His Foot
1954, Bronze
Height: 26 1/2 inches (67.3 cm)
Private Collection, London

Page 13
Paul Cézanne
The Card Players, 1890–92, Oil on canvas
25 3/4 x 32 1/4 inches (65.4 x 81.9 cm)
The Metropolitan Museum of Art, New York
(Bequest of Stephen C. Clark, 1960)

Page 17 (left to right)
Seated Figure (with corrections by Henry Moore)
1951/1952, Charcoal, ink, and wash on vellum
22 x 15 inches (55.8 x 38.1 cm)
Private collection, London

Seated Figure (with corrections by Henry Moore)
1951/1952, Charcoal, ink, wash and white color on vellum
22 x 15 inches (55.8 x 38.1 cm)
Private collection, London

Seated Woman (with corrections by Henry Moore)
1951/1952, Charcoal, pencil and wash on vellum
22 x 15 inches (55.8 x 38.1 cm)
Private collection, London

Seated Man (with corrections by Henry Moore)
1951/1952, Charcoal and pencil on vellum
22 x 15 inches (55.8 x 38.1 cm)
Private collection, London

Page 18 (left to right)
First U.K. one man show at Gimpels Fils Gallery in 1957 where 'Head'
drawing can be seen on the left

Head
1956, Brush and ink
23 3/8 x 18 1/8 inches (59.5 x 46 cm)
Victoria and Albert Museum, London

Pages 70-71
Bull (detail)
1954, Brush, ink and crayon on newsprint
18 1/8 x 23 1/8 inches (46 x 58.6 cm)

Back cover
Terminus
2013, Steel, jarrah wood and frosted raspberry
red Perspex
63 3/8 x 111 x 84 5/8 inches (161 x 282 x 215 cm)

This catalogue was published on the occasion of the exhibition:

ANTHONY CARO

first drawings last sculptures

December 8, 2016 to February 4, 2017

Mitchell-Innes & Nash
1018 Madison Avenue, New York, NY 10075
534 West 26th Street, New York, NY 10001
212 744 7400 www.miandn.com

Plate Photography: Unless otherwise indicated all works illustrated in this catalogue are Courtesy Barford Sculptures Ltd: John Hammond, Mike Bruce, John Goldblatt, Olivia Bax, Marco de Valdivia and Nigel Henderson

Additional Photography:
Page 11 Shigeo Anzai
Page 13 © Metropolitan Museum of Art, New York
Page 18 © Victoria and Albert Museum, London
Page 27 Christopher Burke Studio
Page 35 Ann Igelsrud

Design: Matthew Polhamus
Printing: Phoenix Litho, Philadelphia, PA
Publication director: Cassandra Lozano

ISBN: 978-0-9886188-9-3

Available through DAP/Distributed Art Publishers
155 Sixth Avenue, 2nd floor, New York, NY 10013
Tel: 212 627 1999 Fax: 212 627 9484

Mitchell-Innes & Nash wishes to extend our deepest gratitude to Barford Sculptures Ltd, Paul Caro, Patrick Cunningham, Olivia Bax, Sile Stuttard and Julius Bryant for their support and generosity of spirit without which this exhibition and catalogue would not be possible.